National Press Comments About Mercury's Child

- "Parents take one last go at solving their child's problems by embarking on Mr. Dyer's unique system of behaviour management which turns into a voyage of discovery for them all."

  - The Daily Mirror

- "A behaviour expert with honesty....The message that it was possible to change your life for the better simply by breaking a malign pattern of behaviour made for optimistic, even moving, TV."

  - Janice Turner, **The Radio Times**

- "Within weeks of the parents adopting Mr. Dyer's techniques, the behaviour of their daughter had improved. By the end of seven months their child was having less than two tantrums a month and her special needs diagnosis was being reviewed. Her mother said: 'The change has been incredible. It has all been done without Ritalin. Before I hated her. Now she is a normal child.'"

  - Maxine Frith, **The Independent**

- "Three months on and Warwick's techniques appear to have done the trick. Improvements are noticed at school and at home where Georgina is calmer and more agreeable."

  - The TV Times

GW00645252

- "By the end three dangerously desperate people were beginning to turn themselves into a normal family. Whatever his fee was, Mr. Dyer earned it and then some."
  - Thomas Sutcliffe, **The Independent Review**

- "A humbling, chilling film for any parent to watch."
  - **The Times**

- "Things began to change for the better within only a few days."
  - Peter Paterson, **The Daily Mail**

- "Warwick's methods seem almost too simple to be true, but after a short time Georgina's parents begin to reap the dividend."
  - **The Mail**'s *Weekend Magazine*

- "Mercifully a behaviour expert, Warwick Dyer, was able to work with the couple and break the downward spiral of rage and recrimination."
  - **The Times Magazine**

- "Warwick Dyer, an expert on child behaviour, spots the root of the problem."
  - **The Independent**'s *Information Magazine*

- "Warwick Dyer has created a unique system of child behaviour management."
  - **The Express**

Mercury's Child

Warwick Dyer

This edition is published by Booklocker.com, Inc. for:
Colly.and-Sons co.uk
Colly.and-Sons.co.uk
0 00433106-0
First edition 2005

Thanks for shopping with us.
Kindest Regards, Customer Care

RETURNING GOODS

Please re-pack, in the original packaging if possible, and send back to us at the address below. **Caution!** Don't cover up the barcode (on original packaging) as it helps us to process your return.

We will email you when we have processed your return.

---✂---

PLEASE complete and include this section with your goods.

Your Name: _____

Your Order Number _____

Reason for return _____

Select: Refund my order ☐   Replace my order ☐

(Please note, if we are unable to replace the item it will be refunded.)

Return to:

---✂---

> **RETURNS**
> **Unit 22, Horcott Industrial Estate**
> **Horcott Road**
> **FAIRFORD**
> **GL7 4BX**

Contents

Preface... ix
    Take Your Time and Read Everything ix
    A Book for Parents, Not a Parenting Book x

Introduction... 1
    Why Is There So Much Ineffective Talk?.............. 6

Chapter One 9
    Mercury's Child 9
    Leave Primary Mode Behaviour Behind............... 10
    They Talk Like Us 10
    Mutual Agreement 12
    Compliance Before Agreement............................. 13
    Agree That I Am Right 14
    The Need for Consequences.................................. 16
    Will We Ever Convince Them?............................. 16

Chapter Two... 19
    Democracy Misunderstood 19
    Still Making Up Your Mind.................................. 20

Chapter Three 23
    Mercury's Child—Predictable Behaviour............ 23
    Difference Between Toddlers and Babies.............. 24
    Just Bad Behaviour 26

Chapter Four 29
    What Is Non-Negotiable?...................................... 29

Chapter Five..35
Five Rules for Parents...35
The Most Important Rule in This Book.........................37
Sibling Rivalry..43
Not in Front of the Children..46

Chapter Six...49
Effective Sanctions..49

Chapter Seven...61
The Real World as a Template.....................................61
Rewarding Bad Behaviour..62
Times When You Must Not Try to Make Your Child Feel
Better...63

Chapter Eight..65
If You Are Still Getting Temper Tantrums....................65
The Tantrum—The Ultimate Demand...........................67

Chapter Nine...71
The Seven C's Positive Sanction Method.....................71
The Seven C's...72
Let the Sanction Do the Work.....................................76

Chapter Ten...79
Rewards...79
A Reward-Rich Home..80
A Crazy-Sounding Mantra...82

Chapter Eleven..83
Your Child's Need for Attention..................................83
The Child Can Think or Say ANYTHING.....................84
The Child Is Entitled to a Predicted Future..................86

Chapter Twelve **89**
    Bedtime 89
    The Problem to Tackle First............................... 91
    Gradually Reduce Bedtime 92

Chapter Thirteen.. **93**
    Start Day 93

Chapter Fourteen **97**

Appendix **103**
    The emails in Full 103

Preface

Take Your Time and Read Everything

The behaviour change system described in this book WORKS. I have never had a failure with my fee-paying clients who stuck to it—and nearly all did.

But my clients had daily monitoring from me. You will not.

If you start using the technical strategies in this book without carefully taking in the principles behind them you will not get the changes that you want and will become disillusioned. This system works. It appears simple, but don't throw it all away because you assume that you know what it is getting at without really reading it all. It will make wonderful changes to your family and your life, so don't throw these away by impatiently starting to make these changes **as you are reading it.** If you have a partner **both of you** need to read it, make your own notes, and fully agree what you are going to do. **Only then** set a day to begin your new regime.

I have tried to make it accessible to all parents whatever their educational background but I have not avoided any topic that needed covering, so if through my deficiencies or yours you do not understand what I am getting at, **keep reading.** Later chapters may well explain what you did not understand or agree with earlier. Take your time—read it a second time before you start, just to be sure.

Countless children are trapped in a cycle of bad behaviour. They gain a power in the home that is totally irresistible to them, but which makes them miserable. Parents are completely mystified by what is going on and are equally trapped. All this suffering is quickly and completely reversible. All this is described here with the detail that you need.

A Book for Parents, Not a Parenting Book

Every parent needs to know the techniques explained here and what is happening when behaviour breaks down, but these pages do not provide a model for good parenting. **If your parenting isn't broken, don't fix it**. This book is intended to help you understand and speedily change a spectrum of bad behaviour varying from mild to very serious and then maintain that change.

When I use the inclusive term "we" in the text I do not mean "we parents," but **"We, the parents of children with serious behaviour problems."**

I have already had parents who have only seen the documentaries on UK television—and who have little real information—say that they are using my methods, and I have had a national paper retract an article in which I was quoted as saying that I blame the parents of ADHD children. I have already resigned myself to this book being described as a "back-to-basics" book. **Well, it is not**. Let me state categorically that the main purpose of this book is to encourage parents to **analyse** and avoid **all** polarised views of parenting.

Yes, this is essentially a technical book that will tell you **what to do,** but if you continue to think about your child's behaviour in the same way, it will not change. This book does not tell you to just be more consistent, impose punishments, be stricter. If, when you have finished it, you do not understand the difference between a sanction (punishment) and an "interpersonal sanction," then your child's behaviour will not change.

Once you and your partner have both read this book carefully, sit down and agree on a "Start Day"—a day when you will begin to reclaim your child.

Introduction

The whole aim of this book is to set out for parents of seriously badly behaved children the precise strategies and responses that will quickly transform their child's behaviour. After reading it carefully you will need to decide upon a day to begin your new regime. You can use this book to guide you through the changes as they occur. Start on a particular day by sitting down with all your children, not just the targeted child, and explaining the way things will now be for **all of you**. Parents may well have tried and discarded much advice and many strategies in the past. Much of what was discarded may well have been necessary for any change to occur, but not sufficient by itself to produce the change. This is why I urge you to understand why each of the strategies given here is needed. Each one of them is so important that if you misunderstand or misapply any one of them the house of cards will fall.

There is not a parent anywhere in the world who believes it is a good idea to punish good behaviour and reward bad, but I can tell you this happens all the time.

Scene one
A father and mother, new clients of mine, never agreed about the handling of their son. Their twelve-year-old boy would produce home-wrecking tantrums when he did not get his own way. One evening, after refusing to eat his dinner, he goes out, arguing about the time (8 p.m.) that his mother has insisted he should come back. At 2 a.m. he returns home and rings the bell. The parents already have a sanction (punishment) in place when he arrives home late so the father reminds his wife just to open

the door and come back to bed. The mother opens the door but then prepares something for the boy to eat and chats with him in his room before coming back to bed. The next night the boy refuses to turn the T.V. in his room off even though he has school the next day. His mother tells him that he will lose a portion of his computer time for the time the television stays on, and she leaves his room. He calls her back with, "You have not given me my goodnight kiss." His mother tells him that she has not given him his kiss because the T.V. is still on. He says that she does not really love him, and that all he wants is a kiss. He continues to persuade, and the mother eventually gives him his kiss with the T.V. blaring in the corner of his room.

Scene two
I am standing with a friend in the garden of her house watching her children play when her four-year-old pushes off the top of a slide and deliberately slams into the back or his 18-month-old sister who is yet to clear the bottom. His mother is angry; she takes him aside. "Why did you do that?" she asks. This response is so common and we have heard it used so often that we have probably never thought what a very strange question it is. How is the child supposed to respond? Both of us had seen the deliberation on her son's face when he pushed off with sole intention of hurting his sister. It is not difficult to work out that jealousy was the motive for this behaviour. There is only one honest answer possible: "Because I wanted to," but my friend did not really want to hear the truth; in fact, if the child had said this, my friend would have been horrified.

Scene three
A client of mine, also a behaviour professional, had a 13-year-old daughter with whom he was having serious problems. His daughter's problems were compounded by her refusal to go to

sleep at a reasonable time. Today she is getting herself ready to go to social event at her old primary school and is self-conscious about her appearance as she will be meeting her old primary school friends. She comes to her mother for a dab of make-up to cover a spot on her forehead. Her father chooses this moment to point out that she also has very large dark rings under her eyes.

Many of us only *think* we understand the principles of punishments (sanctions) and rewards.

The parent in the first scene, because of misguided parental instincts and fear of her son's tantrums condones and rewards her son when he breaks her rules. The parent in the second scene thinks an angry question that her child cannot answer honestly is a sanction. In this third scene the father takes the opportunity to score a discipline point and sanction his daughter at a time when she is not behaving badly and when he is most liable to hurt her self-esteem.

Each of these accounts describes responses that will, if not changed, only make the behaviour worse. Each of these parents desperately needs to understand what is wanted so as to appropriately respond to their children in ways that stop bad behaviour **without** harming the child's self esteem.

If we are not clear what to do in response to our children, then bad behaviour can become entrenched and chronic within the family. Our children will suffer because of our lack of clarity, while at the same time they will milk it for all it is worth.

I had been encouraging a client to use small sanctions rather than angry shouting. He told his eight-year-old daughter that she must stop being so rude, saying, "I don't want to take some of your computer time away." She said, "Well if you don't want to take it away, don't do it." Of course, she had not really misunderstood what he meant. She must have understood very well to deliberately misinterpret in this way. Our children are quite capable of understanding our reasons and our rules, but they are also capable of using them against us.

Why is it that they continually search for counter-arguments? Why are they so defiant so much of the time? Why are they so strong-willed that they never seem to tire in their attempts to wear us down? In particular, why do they get so **indignant**? Where on earth does all their **anger** come from?

Look at this list of behaviour problems that parents have told me about in just the last few months. The first comment is about a child of two, and the last is about a child of fifteen—with all the ages in between. (See a larger extract of what they said in Appendix 1)

"He **nags** for hours over anything. He hits me and always says No!"

"She flatly **refuses** to do anything I say. She just refuses to stay in her bed at night."

"My four-year-old is being very rude and **sarcastic** towards us…lashes out."

"When **asked** to do a task, he will only do it if he wants to…screams, throws things."

"My daughter, six, refuses when **told**…had to leave play centre for hitting the teacher."

"My daughter, seven, **interrupts** the teacher when **told** to stop…screams and hits."

"He is **rude and cheeky, says** hurtful things, punches me in passing."

"He does nothing **asked** of him. He steals whatever I will not provide for him."

"My nine-year-old is constantly defiant, **compares** everything I do with her to her sister."

"He **back-talks** at me all the time. He screams and throws things."

"Parenting my 11-year-old is like **working with a politician**. He punches holes in walls."

"She throws really nasty tantrums, then **(when asked)** cannot remember why"

"He is 13, smokes, continues to **ignore** rules and requests. He has low self-esteem."

"My 14-year-old is **verbally abusive** and at times physically aggressive."

"We have stayed off his back like **he has asked**, but at 15 do we allow him to ruin his life?"

Now look at the highlighted words and you will begin to see that the real problem for parents is **not** with their children's behaviour—i.e., what they do— but rather with the negotiations **about** what they do—in other words, the

nagging
refusing
sarcasm
asking
telling
interrupting
rudeness
comparing
back-talking
ignoring
verbal abuse

Why Is There So Much Ineffective Talk?

Talk is at the heart of every one of these problems. These parents have tried asking their children, reasoning with them, nagging them, telling them, shouting at them, only to be met with ignoring, interrupting, rudeness, back-talking, and even louder shouting. Parents have tried distracting them; putting them in "time out" in their rooms; grounding them; taking away toys, privileges, pocket money, food-treats, computer time; and anything else they can think of; even spanking them. Only to be met with even more anger and determination not to change. Nothing works. Why? Well, the answer is a simple one. Many parents just do not realise that when behaviour.has deteriorated badly what the child thinks is happening in these interactions is completely different from what the parents think. Interacting with badly behaved children is effectively like dealing with a different species from a different world. The children have become alien beings in an adult world.

Chapter One

Mercury's Child

Of course all parents know from the beginning that their child is from an alien world. Nothing is as alien as a new baby to new parents. The difference is so clear that it often causes no problems and the parents usually fall hopelessly in love with the tiny new life-form. Without ever seeing their new child they set off on the nine-month return journey to bring the child from Mercury to Earth. The journey involves great hardship and discomfort, but the growing need to save and protect the tiny Mercurian creature drives them both. The life-form is collected and landed safely back on Earth with much joy. The couple are not disappointed but rather amazed by the life-form's strangeness and by how much work and how much tiredness the tiny creature creates.

At first it is easy for them to remember that the tiny being is not at all like them and came from a completely different planet. The creature is so clearly different. It does not talk, but makes noise to communicate its basic needs. Its parents realise their job, if the life-form is to survive, is to provide for these needs. Mercury's baby is a natural dictator—its survival depends on it—and its new parents become its willing slaves.

The life-form's behaviour is seen to be natural. It is clear that this new being has no conception of the adult earth-world and how things function. It cannot speak so cannot ask politely. If it wants something, and at this age it is overwhelmed by the strength of its needs, it has only one method—to demand. This is the first, the primary, state of the relationship between the Mercurian baby and its parents. It is quite natural and quite healthy and, like a light-switch, has only two positions:

"I feel good,"
and,
"I **do not** feel good—I demand—**notice me—make me feel better!**"

Leave Primary Mode Behaviour Behind

Primary Mode behaviour is perfectly healthy and natural for the Mercurian baby, but parents need to gradually train Mercury's child to leave it behind and become an Earth being. Primary Mode behaviour in an older child is very unpleasant to live with, but if we are honest it is not really "bad behaviour"; it is merely immature and misplaced.

They Talk Like Us

Gradually all memory of the child coming from another planet is lost and the problems start. The parents begin to mistakenly assume that the Mercury's child has, or should have, the same way of looking at the world as they do. Earth parents understand that the child has to learn to become an Earth adult, but think this knowledge is gained along with the Earth language. They do not realise that the creature from Mercury still retains his original Primary Mercurian view of the world and that view has to be trained away. Parents need to remember that Mercurian behaviour for a baby is instinctive survival behaviour, which works because **it has to work.** Toddlers have no mechanism for knowing when demanding is no longer needed. They will only leave it behind when it stops working, and if it continues to work they continue the behaviour. Mercury's child has no power to control whether this behaviour is effective; only parents can stop Primary Mode behaviour from working.

The confusion begins when the Mercury's child starts to learn to speak Earth language. The Mercurian way is to demand, and the child needs to be shown by continuous example that asking works but demanding does not. The often-heard entreaty to the toddler, "Say please" is no mere sweet old-fashioned tradition. The parent puts something in between the demand and its supply, the request and its gratification. Here should begin the mantra that parents should hold onto well into the child's teens.

Give them what they want but under your terms.

This is crucial if the child is to leave behind its Primary Mode "demand" behaviour. "Please" and "thank you" mean that a calm non-aggressive action has to be performed **before** the need is met.

Mercury's child continually asks his or her parents for reasons but does not really set much store by them; they are merely words. The child is only really influenced by what actually ends up happening—in other words, **consequences.** Mercury's child may become old enough to be capable of reasoning but will never let words or reason stop him or her from fighting for what he/she wants. Life-forms everywhere survive by controlling consequences. Mercury's children are no different; for them there is only one priority: to get the outcome they want. Coming to Earth and learning how to talk does not change this. If they discover that a particular action brings them what they want **they repeat it**. The Mercurian child is never changed through the use of reason but only by the **very careful control of outcomes**, by giving them predictable **consequences**.

It is not possible to **persuade** Mercury's child of anything. They will never be persuaded that what they want to do at this minute is not in their long-term best interest. They will never accept that they should not **want** to do it. Earth parents often mistakenly think they can persuade their children by **just using words,** and without any other consequence, of the greater **maturity** of the adult Earth view. This is just not possible. Mercury's child only appears to be persuaded by this argument. In reality all he or she can accept is the **inevitability of the outcome**.

Mutual Agreement

Men and women may be from Mars and Venus but children are very definitely from Mercury. They are mercurial, developmentally designed to be interested in **now**—this precise moment. As parents we love our child so much we are sure that they know it. We are sure that they will **understand why** we have to disappoint them. When we have to tell them…

- **now** is the time to go to bed

- no, you **can't have the cake** two minutes before dinner

- you have to stop what you are enjoying and **come in now**

- your homework needs to be **done now**

- what you just said **was rude** and must not be repeated

We are sure they will trust us enough to accept disappointment. But Mercury's children are inexperienced and egocentric. They are never going to be convinced that **our** bedtime for them on a school night is reasonable. It is dishonest to hint that we will ever accept their time since—unless it accords with our own— we will not. Functioning families only **appear** to get mutual agreement in these areas. Mutual agreement in these areas would mean that a child's view had a chance of being accepted even though it was unhealthy or unsafe.

Don't expect them to *want to do it*.
Our children are reluctant to accept our long-term reasons and we often cannot accept their **now** reasons, but when the Mercurian view of the world does not coincide with ours, it is quite possible to get our children to agree **to do it**.

What is not fair or realistic (in fact it is cruel and unnecessary) is to expect them to agree, against all their Mercurian instincts, that they should **want** to do it.

Compliance Before Agreement

It is natural for Earth parents to use reason with their children and to want agreement in areas of dispute. It is right that they explain their reasons to their children, but only up to a point. This desire becomes counter-productive when Earth parents think the child's agreement is **more important** than his or her compliance. The uncomfortable truth is worth repeating that often when Mercury's child **appears** to accept our argument and appears to agree, he or she has just accepted that they cannot **change the outcome**, that the outcome is inevitable.

Look at the difficulties this parent gets into by attempting to get agreement:

My son will be eleven this year. He is not badly behaved at school and doesn't cause his teachers any problems. The problem we have is at home with his defiance! For example, he doesn't think it is fair that he has to do homework, as he works for six hours at school and doesn't see why he has to do more work in his free time (his words!). He finds it difficult to do his homework, and his concentration span is approximately five minutes. If we try to force him to do it we are looking at least an hour or two of battling and then he gets himself in a state and doesn't do it properly anyway.

Agree That I Am Right

After two hours of verbal battling with this Mercurian child, the parent is no nearer to getting this problem resolved. It is clear, since he quotes his son's reasons, that this father wants his son's **agreement.** This is the wrong target, because the words **insist** and **agree** are not compatible. The father cannot insist on something that he wants his son to agree to. He certainly cannot punish his child for **not agreeing**. If agreement is the target, this obstinate child becomes invincible, and the father is stripped of the moral right to provide consequences.

The real target is not agreement but his son's **compliance.** This father has completely failed to make clear what the **consequence** will be if his son does not complete his homework. He can't even mention consequences while he is seeking agreement.

Children in dispute are interested only in outcomes. The outcome for this child is that he has not done his homework properly, which is what he wanted in the first place. So he has got what he wanted **without** any consequence being applied. His father's **angry attention is not punishing**, because attention, even negative attention, is rewarding. Doing or not doing homework should be a **non-negotiable area**, but it is the father, not the son, who continues to negotiate and who has not accepted that homework is non-negotiable, and this is the reason the father is frustrated. He cannot work out if the fault lies with his ability to explain **or** his son's willingness to understand.

Truth is, there is no fault—at least not here. If you look you will see that the father states exactly his son's position, although he does not accept that his son is entitled to **believe this**. This is why the interactions are never-ending. The son is perfectly entitled to believe he should not have to do homework and the father should respect his view. His son is not entitled **not to do it** and only really needs one piece of information from his father—what the consequences will be.

The Need for Consequences

Mercury's child needs consequences. Not only as a means for parents to make sure the adult view of behaviour prevails but because when children are trained to accept small consequences for their own inappropriate behaviour they are being trained to accept—not dwell on—the natural disappointments that life brings without getting angry or blaming others. Without the positive loving application of consequences children will firstly behave badly towards others and secondly will blame others for any disappointment, including those stemming from their own bad behaviour. Without training to accept consequences children revert to—or fail to leave—their Primary Mode behaviour. They continue to say right on into their teenage years and beyond, **"I do not feel good—I demand—make me feel better."**

Will We Ever Convince Them?

Do this father and all parents of defiant children really think that we can persuade those children? When I talk to audiences of parents of seriously misbehaving children I often ask them if they continue with their verbal battles because this is what they want their child to eventually say:

"Oh, yes I see, Dad or Mum, what you are trying to tell me. You want me to do my homework now…. I'm so sorry I did not understand you before, but I now see what you mean! Of course I will do it now and every evening from now on. "

I say this and the response is for all the parents to laugh. It is laughable. There is no way that our children are ever going to say this. Children never ever say this in years of these interactions and the laughter shows that the parents know it. We all know deep down that this is never going to happen. So, why do we keep trying? Do we really think the reason our child does not accept what we are saying is that they need us to explain just that little bit better? Do we really think that, miraculously, the hundredth time it will sink in? Do we really think the problem is in our ability to explain? We must know it is not. The problem is that we are trying to do something completely impossible. We are trying to resolve these disputes **democratically**.

Chapter Two

Democracy Misunderstood

If we know we have the mature view and our child has the immature one, it is natural for us to attempt to persuade our child of the superiority of our view. But trying to get our child to **agree** that only our view is reasonable is not democracy; it is a travesty of democracy. We think that all we need to do is explain and democracy can be preserved. But real democracy has to allow for more than one outcome. If we are really being democratic, we have to allow for the outcome that **we don't want**.

As parents some outcomes have to be non-negotiable. In certain areas only a benign and loving **dictatorship** will provide Mercurian children with the safety and the security they need. We are reluctant to dictate what **must** happen to our children when they are still not accepting our reasons. We are **reluctant dictators**. This makes us vulnerable, because dictatorship is the primary and most natural state for Mercury's child. If the parent does not dictate and take the lead, then the child is more than happy to fill the vacuum.

"If we try to force him to do it, we are looking at least an hour or two of battling, and then he gets himself in a state and doesn't do it properly anyway."

The father equates "an hour or two of battling" with "forcing." Parents often see these long verbal battles as sanctioning (punishing) for the child. This could not be further from the truth. Mercury's children gain confidence from verbal battles because the angry dialogue tells them that all is not lost and they may still get their own way. It enables them to use their main Mercurian attribute—**never giving up**. This father wants his son to perform the **physical action** of homework, but has spent nearly two hours talking about the **principal** of whether or not he should **want** to do it.

Still Making Up Your Mind

He ends up fighting two battles when he should only be fighting one. He wants the child to comply **and** agree father is right. All he should want is for the child to **comply.** There is no point in battling to change the son's beliefs. There is no contest between Mercury's child's beliefs and what he or she wants. Even if children secretly agree with us they will **rarely** admit it. However determined we are to convince them we are right we never will. We cannot use will-power to get agreement—what sort of agreement would that be? Neither should we attempt to use too much will-power to get compliance, not if it creates this pattern:

Will-power attempting to stop the child from doing X = continuous talking about X = continuous attention for child doing X = continuous reward for X.

Attention is the child's biggest reward, bar none. The will-power of Mercury's child is far superior to any that Earth parents can muster. If Primary Mode behaviour gets minimal attention and never works, the child will quickly leave it behind. A never-ending cycle of explaining will not convince the child of your point of view. In fact, going on and on trying is disrespectful, since we are suggesting the child is **not entitled** to his or her view. Children's views are real for them and they are entitled to their views, although they are not entitled to have their views **succeed**. We are a long way from democracy when we refuse to allow our child a view that differs from our own. Children's views are Mercurial and immature, but it is **their** view from their planet. So, let them have their own views, firstly out of respect for them, but secondly out of self-interest.

When parents continue to discuss the differences between the child's view and their own about, say, why the child **should go to bed now**, a massive area of doubt and insecurity is created. Why? Because parents think that they are trying to explain a decision that has already been made, but the **act of discussing** convinces the child the decision has not yet been made. **Discussion makes a child think the decision can still be changed.** Every moment parents spend discussing a categorical decision it becomes less and less categorical. By responding, by all this nagging, reasoning, asking, interrupting, telling, we think we will convince the child of the rightness of the decision we **have made**. But all this indicates to the child that the decision has not yet been made, and that we are **still making up our minds.**

Chapter Three

"Bad behaviour" is always "interactional." Without a parent-figure to interact with it is impossible for a child to behave badly. Children need their parents as a foil, an audience, and a reward for their bad behaviour. All "bad behaviour" is essentially **Primary Mode** behaviour, with the child interacting with the parent in a way that was once perfectly natural but is now out of place.

Parents rightly respond and calm their babies. It is always right to comfort a baby; a baby that is distressed or in pain will not "cry itself to sleep." Allowing a baby to scream is to risk an unnecessary battle in which the baby may start choking or go blue and force us to reward an **escalation** in their distressed behaviour. We should never train our baby that showing increased distress will force us to attend to them.

Comforting a distressed baby is **always** right (this does not always mean picking the baby up; in fact holding a very tired baby is often not a good idea). It means using our voice or motion to soothe and calm, gradually doing less and less. By giving the baby what it wants we strive to control the interactions so that the baby will become less demanding.

23

Difference Between Toddlers and Babies

Toddlers also need, as much as is possible, to be given what they want; however, there is an important difference. They can now indicate what they want, but they can't always have it. It is at this point that parents can make the serious mistake of trying to do more than be sympathetic when the child is disappointed. Mercury's child needs to be helped to ask politely for what they can have and cope with the disappointment for what he or she can't have. Toddlers occasionally need a kindly "no," and to be constantly reminded to say "please." Without gentle training to accept disappointment, the child cannot help but retain its Primary Mode behaviour. Once it is mobile we cannot afford for children to feel that they can change a "no" into a "yes," or that parents will attempt to "make up for" an unavoidable disappointment. If we do, we also train them to always blame someone else when they are disappointed. The resulting children have remarkably similar characteristics:

Mercury's children
- get into a temper if they are not getting their own way
- seem not to be able to understand reasons or logical explanations
- are defiant
- won't listen to you, or talk over you when you are trying to explain
- are strong-willed; tend to wear you down

They also
- find it difficult or impossible to lose, even over small unimportant things

- tend to blame others for even small disappointments

When you attempt to punish them they will
- say they "don't care"
- threaten or produce a temper tantrum or other retaliation
- say you are unfair
- try to make you feel guilty
- say you don't love them
- say they don't like or love you

They may also
- appear to be selfish
- tend to argue with or be spiteful to brothers or sisters
- tend to be spiteful to you, or say hurtful things
- tend to whine or complain
- often need a lot of reassurance
- have tendency to demand affection when they don't deserve it
- occasionally still be sleeping in their parent's bed

Interactive behaviour problems do not always appear to affect relationships outside the home but when they do, these children
- tend not to have or not keep friends
- tend to have friends like themselves or younger friends
- tend to have friends they can dominate

These children may not have problems at school but when they do, they
- may have problems with peers at break times
- may take a strong dislike to and get in trouble with new or particular teachers

The above characteristics usually mean
- the child is usually very powerful within the family with a strong will that may be overpowering
- the child usually has very low self-esteem and is unhappy much of the time

Just Bad Behaviour

These children are just behaving badly, yet this list of characteristics looks as serious as any of the lists of symptoms of major disorders like ADHD or Asperger's Syndrome or Attachment Disorder. In fact some behaviour on this list can become so extreme it is hard to believe it is just "bad behaviour," and parents and professionals can be fooled. You would not expect a child that was just badly behaved to

- seem not to be able to understand reasons or logical explanations

- find it difficult or impossible to lose, even over small unimportant things

- tend to blame others for even small disappointments

- occasionally still be sleeping in their parents' bed

- tend not to have or not keep friends

- usually have very low self-esteem and be unhappy much of the time

Intuitively we would not expect these to be the result of "bad behaviour." The Mercurian child is very powerful within the family with a strong will that is often overpowering, yet the characteristics above do not describe a child with a positive self-concept or one that is emotionally "strong." The child these characteristics describe is lonely and insecure. These children are not emotionally unable to accept loss or small disappointments—they just have not learnt to do it. They see small disappointments as a personal affront. Mercury's child is caught in this terrible paradox created by parents....

The less convinced they are that parents value and love them, the more convinced they are that they have to "win." Yet "winning" itself, and their parents' reaction to it, convinces them that parents don't value and love them.

Disappointment is part of life and cannot be controlled. The sun goes down and the children's party has to come to an end. We have to go to bed. We have to get up to go to school or work. Others can afford things that we can't. Not all our desires can be met.

Luckily it is never too late and is often quite easy to train a youngster to accept loss without overreaction, provided parents **never** modify outcomes in a child's favour in response to overreaction. Children, however badly behaved, are not fools; they will not learn to change any behaviour that works. When they are absolutely clear that negotiation is not happening and an outcome cannot be changed, they will **always** accept it.

Chapter Four

What Is Non-Negotiable?

Are we always clear in our own minds exactly what is non-negotiable?

The father of the son with the homework problem quotes his son's remarks and you sense that he secretly thinks that his son has a point, and of course, from the boy's Mercurian perspective, he does. Does the fact that the boy has a point alter the strength of the father's categorical statement, "Johnny, it's six o'clock—it's time to do your homework now."? Does it make this statement any less categorical? The answer has to be "no."

No grey areas
The reason is a simple one. Our statements need to be
100% categorical, non-negotiable
or
100% free choice
and never the twain shall meet—with never any grey areas.

Either the child has a genuine choice and the parent accepts that choice happily, or the parent's view is 100% categorical and unchangeable. It is unfair to the child if there are any grey areas or any doubts. Disputes are always repeated and these grey areas are always the reason. Some parents actually use the interactions with their children to make up their minds. This means that every decision, not just the current one, is "up for

29

grabs." Parents can avoid pointless discussion and provide consequences only if the parents are absolutely clear and precise about what is non-negotiable.

"Right, I have had enough"
We have to decide what is not acceptable beforehand. Otherwise it can easily become dependent upon how we are feeling. What you can put up with today may be very different tomorrow; your tolerance levels will vary. "I have had enough" is not the basis for a consistent response and will create children more concerned with their parents' mood than their own behaviour.

Cheeky chappy
Many times I have seen a smile appear on the faces of parents when they describe something outrageous that their child has done or said. I always point out that they have to **decide**: either their child is a "cheeky chappy" and his or her actions humorous and good-natured, **or** the behaviour is serious and needs to change. They cannot have it both ways. If the child sees a smile, our chance of changing the behaviour will be nil. Getting serious about it afterwards will just create a massive mixed message. Parents cannot reward the behaviour **and** expect the child to leave it behind.

Your categorical circle
I ask parents to draw a circle and write inside it those things that their child should **not** decide. The list of things that parents put inside their circle needs to be personal to them, but these lists usually look very much the same. Parents are always surprised how short the list is. In fact inside the parents' circles there are usually just four words:

- **Health** - time of going to bed, eating appropriately, doctor and dentist decisions

- **Safety** - decisions about what is dangerous, what the children play with, where they go, what they do, who they are with, the time they should return

- **Education** - application at school, homework
  (some parents will want to include religious education)

  (Some parents include **Housework** (often token) and help around the house, but this is optional—"clearing up after yourself" and "helping out" are important but are probably best included in the fourth area below)

The forth word is one that I always insist parents include. In the early days of my work I felt a little guilty about it. I thought its inclusion was to do with my age and my upbringing. I thought perhaps it was old-fashioned, not really important for modern families. I soon realised that this word was actually so crucial that without its constant application to every single moment of the child's day NONE of the changes that parents crave are possible.

The word is

- **Politeness** - social skill - sharing

Politeness and social skill are central, because rudeness is a public denial of the parents' leadership. If a child is even slightly rude, parents' efforts to change behaviour will take much longer and may not succeed at all. Politeness is the crucial indicator of the child's move away from Primary Mode behaviour, away from Mercury towards Earth.

Rudeness and self-esteem

While children are being rude to parents they are seriously undermining **their own** sense of self-worth. Pride in our parents is usually our first sense of pride. Inability to stop continuous rudeness will eventually begin to make the children lose respect for their parents and, along with it, respect for themselves. Chronic rudeness creates an emotionally negative communication style which makes the child question whether the parents like/love them. Lack of ability to notice or stop the rudeness undermines the parent in their child's eyes—cheapening the parent merely serves to cheapen their own predicted worth; their model of who they feel they will become. On so many levels it is **vital that parents make politeness/ rudeness non-negotiable.**

Health - Safety - Education - Politeness

So there are just these four areas that are non-negotiable. Parents need to be absolutely clear which decisions are off-limits for discussion. They need to give reasons clearly and say they are not going to discuss them further; discussion will not help the child to accept those reasons. Parents must completely put out of mind all thought of repeatedly explaining or trying to persuade. Youngsters need a choice between following the instruction and a practical sanction or consequence if they refuse.

No Mercurian child will ever be **persuaded** of the importance of the words in your circle.

Health

Safety

Education

Politeness

Chapter Five

Five Rules for Parents

If parents want to gain control of the four non-negotiable areas above they desperately need rules or aims of their own that will prevent them being drawn into irritable discussion. There are just five rules or aims that parents need to follow that will prevent all the heartache that Mercurial children cause:

1. Strive for compliance, NOT agreement.
(In categorical areas)
We hope we have explained this rule in the first two chapters.

2. Never introduce rewards and sanctions for just one child.
With all of Mercury's children that I have worked with over the years, two words come to mind: *Power* and *Isolation*. Badly behaved children are tremendously powerful within families, but lonely and isolated. Their behaviour will never change while they remain on the outside, and a major goal for parents is to help them rejoin their own family. Anything parents do in isolation to a particular child adds symbolically to this separation, and deprives that child's brothers and sisters of a structure that they invariably also need. Interventions from outside, however worthy, initially increase the child's sense of power and isolation, making him or her more special and more alone. Intervention techniques that are general to the family are always to be preferred, particularly since parents, once a

specific child's problems decrease, become more aware of the behaviour of brothers and sisters.

Rule three

The third rule (below) again brings us back to rudeness. Parents often don't take rudeness seriously because they think that it is merely a symptom of their lack of control of their children. In fact rudeness is **the main cause** of their lack of control.

Why are children rude?

It is natural for children to want their own way but it is not natural for them to be rude, so why are they? Rudeness is not, as some parents think, the result of a personality flaw in the child, and it has nothing to do with the child's strong will or angry nature. Children are rude for one reason only: because being rude **works**. They are rude because without realising it we have trained them that if they are rude we are **more** likely to listen to them and **more** likely to respond to their comments. The fact that rudeness makes parents angry is a small price to pay if parents are listening and taking the child seriously. Parents nearly always respond to points made rudely, so Mercury's child uses rudeness to emphasise the point he or she is making. Children quickly realise that rudeness **actually helps them** get attention and get their own way.

So the third rule (below) is vital. Its **constant** application will often train away rudeness in a few weeks, sometimes in days. We are very lucky, because Mercury's child is only interested in **effective** methods for getting what he or she wants and is rarely interested in rudeness for its own sake. If rudeness stops working, Mercury's child stops being rude. The third rule enables us to show children that they are **less** likely to be heard and **less** likely to get a reply if they are rude.

The Most Important Rule in This Book

That is why this third rule is the most important rule in this book....

3. Answer the rudeness, not the point being made.
(Correct the rudeness; don't reply to the point.)

Keeping to this rule is crucial but, at first, very difficult. Arguments loudly and rudely made by our children are very, very seductive. Even when we have accepted that prolonged discussions with our children are fruitless, rudeness will quickly seduce us into a response. Our children are brilliant at drawing us into discussion. They accuse us rudely; they rudely and deliberately misunderstand us; they challenge us rudely; they contradict us rudely. We are "sucked into" responding, not to their rudeness, but to their point. After a while we do not even notice the way our children speak to us. We miss the **way** they speak to us, and spring to defend and explain ourselves.

If we stop concentrating on what our children say and focus on the way they say it, their rudeness quickly becomes ineffective and disappears and with it their main means of undermining us. The self-control needed by parents to achieve this is massive. This third rule tells us we must **never** address the issue being raised if the child is rude. For instance, if the child shouts rudely,

"Where's my shirt?"

we reply politely,

"Holly, that sounds rude, darling. I can't answer you if you shout at me."

Alternatively, give them the words and the tone that they **should have used;** children often have no idea what that tone sounds like…so respond by modelling the words for them….

"Mum, can you tell me where my shirt is, please?"

The child will know that the parent wants him or her to repeat the question with their words. At first he or she is likely to repeat it sarcastically. Being sarcastic is rude—so, again, we gently point out that this is still rude and that the child needs to be polite if he or she wants our help. If the child cannot ask appropriately even with prompting (and they won't at first) then we **cannot even listen to what they want**—we need to stick to this rule and not waver from it from the very beginning of our new regime, and we need to use sanctions (explained in Chapters 6 and 9) to support the rule. We don't make allowances because this is the first time we have insisted on this; children need to know right from the start that even a little rudeness will no longer work. From the moment the new regime starts we will need to turn this tap off completely. Parents often get angry **and** respond to what has been said— when they should do neither. If our child refuses to stop the rudeness, a warning should be given and then a small sanction politely imposed. This rule is so important that it applies even when it is the **parent that wants something**, even when we want to explain something crucial to our child. If the child is rude we still stop and politely indicate that they are being rude and what the consequence will be if they interrupt or make more rude comments. Parents need to stay calm. If worst comes to worst, stop; we can warn the child that there will be an extra sanction if he or she does not allow us to finish. The point we are trying to make will, in any case, be completely undermined if we continue while they are being rude.

Train away whining

This same rule applies to constant whining. Parents should give their child a demonstration of how the same complaint or problem can be communicated without the whining tone. Children whine because it "cuts through" and is **more** effective at getting a response.

A style of communication

If we want to change chronic bad behaviour—tantrums, rudeness, constant whining—it is best not to think of them as bad behaviours at all. It is much more accurate and much more productive to think of them as a **communication style** or even an embryonic and developing **attitude toward life**. Some children never talk—they always whine. Whining cuts through. It works. The child hits upon behaviours that are guaranteed to get attention, but which depend for their power on being unremittingly negative.

So this third rule—answer the rudeness, **not** the point being made—is without doubt and by far the most important rule in this book. It is by the relentless but warm and calm use of this rule that we will reclaim our child and our child's trust in us and his or her trust in life.

Rule Four

If we look even more closely at our conversations with our children, we will arrive at our fourth rule. Parents often get very angry and do a lot of "telling off," yet despite this their children do not end up with any **tangible** consequence for refusal or rudeness.

The fourth rule is….

4. Provide concrete consequences; don't get angry.
   (Don't "tell them off" or try to persuade.)

This rule is massively important. Why is it that many parental responses don't work? Why is it that so many things parents do in response to bad behaviour make things dramatically worse? The answer is that concrete responses are effective but emotional responses make things worse. We may get the first bit right and make it clear to our children what the sanction will be and what they need to do to avoid it, but if this information is given **in conjunction with** an angry emotional message then it is this message that is taken up, copied and mirrored back by the child.

Lack of control over our own feelings at these times is a main cause of chronic bad behaviour. We can completely reverse the effects of our sanctions and rewards by the emotions we allow to be associated with them. If there is a choice between what we say and **what we do** children will always be influenced most by how we act. Showing Mercury's child that you, too, are an angry child just beneath the surface is a very strong message. If the parent giving the sanction is angry, the child is angry in return—and **less inclined** to be influenced by the sanction.

This is the reverse of what parents think. As parents, we think that if we are angry we are showing our determination. We too, like our children, attempt to use anger for emphasis. We think that being angry is the same as being "strict," when in reality it just waters down our sanction. It just encourages the child into constant battling with us, which in turn leads them to fundamentally doubt how we really feel about them. Badly behaved children desperately need reassurance, but our anger just makes them strive for the next best thing—negative attention.

<u>Removing blame</u>
Parents often blame the child for the child's behaviour. This inclination is understandable given the horrendous things that children can do. Parents think they have tried everything, but they need to accept that Mercury's child is always **blameless**. If parents believe children are to blame for their behaviour, a combative style of training becomes almost inevitable. When parents are able to see how quickly a child's behaviour changes when parents do the right things, they realise that it can never have been right to blame the child. It makes no difference if the child is predisposed to behave badly by a behaviour disorder or behaves badly due to the parents' own past deficiencies; **blame is always unfair**. When parents see that changes in their responses are working, it is easier for them to accept this. The hardest time, and parents need to be prepared for it, is when they are striving to respond appropriately but their child **has not yet** begun to change. If parents are doing it right they **must keep going**.

<u>The behaviour, not the child</u>
It is vital that parents focus their dissatisfaction solely on the behaviour, **not the child.** It is this distinction that makes the behaviour-change method in this book effective. Parents need to make this distinction during every conversation and every interaction. The child is always **all right** and the parent-child relationship always sacrosanct. It is always the behaviour **alone**

that is not right and needs to change and always the behaviour that is sanctioned. If we sanction the behaviour it will tend to decrease; if, however, we use an "interpersonal sanction"— which tells the child we are dissatisfied with him or her **as a person**—then we lower self-esteem, create reciprocal anger, and nullify our sanctions. Tangible consequences are essential, and they have a major additional spin-off in that they help parents avoid "interpersonal sanctions" and blame.

We don't talk of consequences

After I gave a speech at a major UK parenting charity the chairperson told me she was particularly interested in my speech because "our charity takes a positive approach to parenting" and "does not deal in consequences or sanctions." I pointed out that it is impossible to avoid sanctions, and that when a previous speaker had talked of breaking down in tears of despair and anger in front of her boy, she had been describing a powerful "sanction." Despair and anger are powerful interpersonal sanctions, which, because they harm the child's self-esteem and increase the child's sense of power, make "bad behaviour" worse. Sanctioning is inevitable; it is **impossible to avoid it**, so it makes sense to do it well and not use "interpersonal" sanctions. It makes sense not to show our children how much we disapprove of their losing control and getting angry by losing control or getting angry **ourselves**.

We need to *demonstrate the emotion that we want and not copy the emotion we are getting.*

The father with the homework problem would have benefited from this advice; he said, *"If we try to force him to do it we are looking at least an hour or two of battling and then he gets himself in a state and doesn't do it properly anyway."*

It is probably not just the child that is getting "in a state" here. This father equates angry words and "telling off" with "forcing," and probably thinks that these function like a punishment (sanction). Angry words do not function like a sanction; parental anger is a great way of getting attention, but it encourages rudeness and creates more opposition and a very poor training environment. In fact, the parent's angry words act far more like a reward than a sanction; they keep the behaviour going. They tell the child he is still being listened to and that there is still a chance his view may succeed. It becomes a contest to see who can be more obstinate and forceful, and this is a contest that Mercury's child is tailor-made to win. If you want to stop your child from continually getting angry, is vital that you don't **join in**.

Sibling Rivalry

<u>The Fifth Rule</u>
The fifth rule (below) is vital if you want to stop continual arguments and fights between your children.

My daughter and I had recently arrived at a birthday party for one of her school friends. She was feeling a little shy, not yet ready to join in, and was standing next to my chair in a quieter room adjoining the main party room. There were only a few people in the room; opposite me was a mother, with a boy of about nine and a girl of about seven. In the middle of the room was an old-fashioned polished wood table on which had been placed an enormous bowl of sweets for the children. The boy asked his mother if he could take one. The mother said that yes, he could. He picked up one of the sweets. Immediately his sister said,

"Oh, Mummy, I wanted that one."

Their mother was confused. It was clear that something was making it difficult for her to know what to say. If you have children you will not be surprised by her confusion or the reason for it. The bowl in question contained probably 200 sweets, all of which were barley sugar. All were the same flavour and colour and with wrappings all the same. It was clear that the reason her daughter "wanted that one" had nothing to do with sweets.

This mother is searching for that magic response that will square the circle and keep everybody happy. She avoids telling an intelligent child that it is **more** sensible to take one of the 200 identical sweets from the bowl. You do not have to be a genius to realise that this dispute has nothing to do with sweets. The attraction of the sweet in her brother's hand has nothing to do with the sweet itself and everything to do with the fact that it was **in her brother's hand**. This story is obviously about the rivalry between the two children, and the other 200 sweets in the bowl waiting to be picked make this clear. Although it is not usually as clear as this, nearly all of the disputes between children are based on this same rivalry. There are very few genuine disputes between children—i.e., both genuinely deciding to do or want exactly the same thing at the same time—and these are easily prevented with simple rules. **Real disputes, real issues, are not the reason children argue**.

What are they rivals for?
The children in my story and all arguing children everywhere are not really rivals for tangible things—sweets, etc.—they are

rivals for their parents' **support.** This is the only reason children consistently argue and it becomes a problem—because parents think that the way to handle disputes is to arbitrate. The problem with arbitration is that it produces a child **with** the parents' endorsement and a child **without it** and it does this **every** time. Clearly both children want their parents to prove them right and—even more important—prove their brother or sister wrong. Should the girl in the story end up with her brother's sweet, then she has gained nothing apart from support. It is clear that this is the only reason she has manufactured this dispute. There is no limit to the number of disputes that can be crammed into a day when their aim is the simple satisfaction of being judged right.

$$A \leftrightarrow B$$

Arbitration
Parents must avoid arbitration at all costs. Let us imagine a clear-cut case where child A has punched child B without provocation. (In practice where children are in constant dispute no incident is clear-cut). The parent arbitrates and decides that child A is at fault, and he or she is "told off" or receives some sanction. A, whether his punch was provoked or not, was already angry with B or he would not have hit him. Undoubtedly A now feels even angrier with B because B has been supported while A has been "told off."

So A, **having lost**, wants to fight again.

B, having won his parents support, has enjoyed beating A and is keen to repeat the whole process. **Having won**, B wants to fight again.

Arbitration always leaves both youngsters eager for their next confrontation. Parents need to rethink what the "bad behaviour" actually is. The "bad behaviour" is not what A or B did but the fact that they were **both** arguing or fighting. Sanctions should be used on **both children** equally for both being part of the dispute and not for one or other of the children for **not being right** at that particular moment.

Not Fair
Parents are naturally reluctant to sanction the child that they see as blameless together with the child that they think is at fault, but parental arbitration for basic sibling disputes stops children from learning how to compromise. Not using this strategy, which is capable of stopping these constant arguments within a few weeks, is even more unfair to both children.

So the fifth rule is,

5. Don't arbitrate (sanction them both equally for the dispute).

Not in Front of the Children

This brings us to our sixth and last rule:

6. Support each other in front of the children.

Parents do not just undermine their partners' authority if they criticise or second-guess his or her decisions in front of the child; they also seriously undermine their own. If two parents are not sure which approach is right, why should their child take any notice of **either view?** Parents need to support all of each other's actions and decisions, whether right or wrong, in front of the children. Once either parent has spoken it becomes law until both parents have a chance to speak privately and resolve any differences for the future. If parents don't do this their views may become polarised, with one parent becoming increasingly conciliatory and the other increasingly hard-line.

So, to recap, we have just five rules for governing our interactions with our badly behaving children:

1. **Strive for compliance, NOT agreement.**
2. **Never introduce rewards and sanctions for just one child.**
3. **Answer the rudeness, not the point being made.** (Correct the rudeness or whining; don't reply to the point.)
4. **Provide concrete consequences; don't get angry.** (Demonstrate the emotion you want; don't copy the emotion you are getting.)
5. **Don't arbitrate.** (Don't try to work out who to support and who to punish; teach the missing social skills involved, and sanction **the argument, i.e., both children.**)
6. **Support each other in front of the children.** (Support all actions and decisions of the other parent whether right or wrong, **even if the other parent's action breaks one of the first four rules or any other rules in this book.**)

Chapter Six

Effective Sanctions

Effective sanctions are incremental; they are able to be given a little bit at a time.

I watch a seven-year-old in a classroom refusing to do anything he is asked, pushing other children onto the floor because they have something he wanted, sweeping everything on the teachers desk onto the floor with his arm as a way of punctuating his latest refusal. From registration to first break, as I watch, he causes almost continual mayhem. This boy is very lucky—he has a very good teacher. Both she and I are determined to prevent the move to special school for the boy, which at this point is only weeks away. We are both searching desperately for some means to help him control his behaviour. I ask his teacher if there is anything the boy really likes.

"Oh yes," she says, "he loves swimming." (The class has a 30-minute swimming lesson each week.)

I suggest that perhaps we could use the loss of swimming as the incentive, and the teacher tells me that she has already tried this and that it does not work. I ask her why. She says,

"I try to hold off and not take his swimming away but the warnings do not seem to work and eventually I have to actually take it away."

49

"What happens then?"

"His behaviour becomes far worse."

It became clear to us that we had to avoid the complete loss of swimming. This boy's enjoyment of swimming was a powerful resource, but once the privilege of swimming was completely lost, his behaviour was worse. It was clear that sanctions needed to be used a little at a time so teachers or parents wouldn't "run out." We decided to take 30 seconds of swimming away if the boy refused to follow an instruction, but then we soon realised that his behaviour was so extreme this would still mean that he would lose his swimming. He could easily have 60 sanctions in a day, let alone a week. We needed to add to our main rule,

1. Don't run out of (or use up) our sanction, a second and third rule:

2. Always give the child **a warning**, a chance for the child back down before we sanction, and,

3. Always have a clear bottom limit in our heads and whatever the child does, never allow ourselves to go lower than the limit—i.e., even if we are taking the reward away a little at a time, never take all of the reward away. (Of course you do not let your child know about this rule.)

How Children Control Their Own Consequences

However, even if we don't allow our sanctions to run out, we still have a problem. Every child needs to be taught about the inevitability of consequences, but Mercury's child has developed strategies designed to prevent us from providing sanctions. We need to be able to anticipate and counter these strategies.

Badly behaved children are usually not as out-of-control as they appear. Before they enact even really serious, apparently emotionally driven behaviour, they have calculated the likely outcome. It is really easy for them to do this, because **they know what happened last time.** Children do not enter the bad behaviour tunnel without being able to see clear light at the end. Avoiding unwanted consequence is a crucial part of their calculation.

Children control their own consequences
You have told your child the particular behaviour is not acceptable and have gotten to the stage where you have told him or her that a particular sanction will be used if they do not comply. They have refused, so you tell them the sanction has now been imposed. Now your child sees it as his or her job stop the sanction from happening, or to undermine your faith in that sanction for the future. All their strategies have just one goal— **to create doubt.** To make you
- doubt if the sanction will work
- doubt if the sanction is worth the confusion it will cause
- doubt about whether your child will ever stop complaining—can you hold out?
- doubt about whether the sanction is fair or too harsh
- doubt about whether you said what you thought you said
- doubt if the child is actually to blame
- doubt about whether the sanction is still necessary as they are now saying they will behave

- doubt about how serious the behaviour was as now they are apologising or joking or being charming
- doubt about how quickly you should comfort them (they are acting as if your sanction has made them **so** distressed)

Let us look at each of the strategies in turn:

1. Saying "I don't care."
The first ploy used by Mercury's child is designed to make you doubt if the sanction will work. The classic response to any sanction is to say, "I don't care" or to act as if they don't care. If you believe your child does not care—as in, "Take all my pocket money, I don't care," you are unlikely to use this pocket money consequence again and may well end up throwing away a really effective sanction.

A parent told me recently,

"The real problem is punishment; no punishment really bothers him. I am reluctant to send him to his room, as he says he does not care, or at night it can make him anxious and he is frightened of going upstairs on his own or sleeping in his own room. I have tried making him sit in a chair and not moving for 10 minutes, but this doesn't bother him either. He even told the psychology team that he enjoys it as it's boring."

This parent has obviously not read the children's story *The Briar Patch;* if he had he would have known that children use exactly the same strategy as Brer Rabbit in the children's story:

Brer Fox catches his hated enemy Brer Rabbit and tells him that he is going to tear off his ears and eat them. Brer Rabbit

52

says, "I don't care about my ears, Brer Fox, so long as you don't fling me in that there briar patch."

Brer Fox is taken aback; how can he punish Brer Rabbit with something that the rabbit does not care about? He changes tack and says that he is going to tear out Brer Rabbit's eyes and eat them. But Brer Rabbit says, "I don't care about my eyes, Brer Fox, but please don't throw me in the briar patch."

You probably already see the point. Brer Fox goes on and on changing his threats of punishment, only to be told that Brer Rabbit does not care, until Brer Fox finally gives Brer Rabbit the punishment that the rabbit **says** he really dreads—only to be told (from a safe distance!),

"Born and bred in the briar patch Mr. Fox, born and bred!"

Children do not have to know this story—their strong desire not to lose naturally makes them pretend not to care. They may then begin to notice that this pretence has the bonus that their parents never stick to any sanction.

2. "If you punish me I'll punish you."
The second ploy used by Mercury's child is to make you doubt if the sanction is worth the confusion it will cause. The usual means is the temper tantrum.

Children threaten and often carry out their threats to have a tantrum, or break something, or harm themselves, or harm their parents. Parents get so concerned with stopping the tantrum that they often allow the child's intimidation to succeed. They forget to provide small consequences for each rude, destructive, or dangerous act within the tantrum. Staying calm yourself and providing consequences are the very first priority if you want to stop tantrum behaviour; getting the child to calm down **must come second** (safety permitting). It is only if this intimidation "works" that children continue to have temper tantrums—they are rarely as out of control as they seem.

Give in before
Parents who are likely to "give in" need to do so **before** they are pressured, **before** the intimidating behaviour is threatened. Once it is even hinted at, it is too late. "Give me what I want or else" is Mercury's child desperately holding on to the baby's Primary Mode behaviour. It only continues if parents "give in" when the child has made a demand—not a request—or after the parent has already told the child "no." The demands of Mercury's child will increase in unreasonableness and violence right through adolescence and beyond if parents continue to reward this behaviour. The temper tantrum is often so difficult to handle that I have devoted Chapter 8 to it.

3. Trying to tire you out / wear you down
Mercury's child wants to make you doubt your own resolve as he or she pleads or complains on and on and on, continuously. The length of time the child continues to question your decision is almost mathematically determined by the length of time it took for you to back down **last time**. The rule *Answer the rudeness, not the point being made* can be very useful here because the child is usually very rude as well as very persistent so you can correct and sanction the rudeness and show, at the same time, that you are not going to negotiate.

4. Attempting to make you feel guilty
Mercury's child wants to make you have doubts about whether the sanction is too harsh. Classically they say, "it's not fair";

they sulk and complain; they demonstrate how bad or angry you are making them feel; they say, "you don't love me," or "I don't love you," or "I hate you," or that you are "bad parents."

5. Questioning what you said the rule really was

Mercury's child wants to make you doubt that you said clearly what the rule was. They will swear blind that what you actually said was, surprise, just what they want to happen now. You need to make sure that they are clear both about the sanction and the exact point when it is to be imposed. This is another reason to warn them, tell them clearly that this is the last chance, and tell them the exact point when the sanction will be applied if they do not comply. This will not stop them from saying they did not understand or that you are being unfair, but **you will be sure** that they did and you are not.

6. Lying—saying they didn't do it

On of my clients recently wrote,

"The other big mistake that you helped us with was our tendency to believe him when a little thought and a few questions would have shown he was not telling the truth. I thought unconditional love was important and taking his side was a facet of this. The trouble is, it trained Paul to be an excellent liar, knowing that he could lie to us, we would take his side and being bright articulate people, we could generally get him, or let him, off the hook. Unfortunately there comes a point where we can no longer do this."

Of course, if the excuse is plausible we must take the trouble to check it out, but it astonishing how many parents are convinced that children will not lie to them and do not bother to check excuses that are completely implausible. Well, here's the thing: Any child who knows we will not check will lie. For Mercury's child, morality comes a very poor second to winning and getting his or her own way. Take the time to make sure. Clearly, if we really cannot be sure, then we cannot sanction, but Mercury's child will often admit to other things that can also be sanctioned, and these are usually plenty. For instance, if the child says that the picture broke in the middle of a tantrum "by accident" then give them a sanction for angry/rude behaviour and not being careful.

7. Saying they will behave well now (if you don't impose the sanction—give them another chance)
Mercury's child wants to make you doubt about whether the sanction is still necessary as he or she is now saying that they will behave. Unfortunately, if you take away the sanction that you warned them about they will have "gotten away with it," and their newly found behaviour will not last long. If you have sanctioned them fairly (see Chapter 9), you will have already given them another chance **before** you finally imposed the sanction.

8. Trying to charm or joke to undermine your seriousness
Mercury's children want to make you have doubts about how serious the behaviour was. They become very helpful, and they use charm and smiles and humour. They try to make you laugh, try to make you change your mood. They count on your sanction not being firmly based on their refusal, which they cannot change, but on **how you feel about** their refusal, which they can change. You gave them a chance already, which they didn't take, so don't fall for this one.

9. Expecting warmth from you too soon and apologies under their terms

Mercury's children want to make you have doubts about whether or not they should be treated lovingly following a tantrum or an apology. They insist on asking—too early—for expressions of warmth, kisses, hugs, cuddles, or they act as if the problem is mutual and forgiveness mutual, as if you and they are "making up." They find this ploy far easier to do if you have in fact lost your temper and really do feel guilty.

Apologies can be a trap.

One of my clients who had serious problems with her sons (11 and 13) told me about a terrible day with them on a trip to Hampton Court. The boys from the outset were uncooperative and spent the day being rude and abusive, refusing to move when asked to, or respond when spoken to, demanding ice-cream and treats, snatching these if they were brought, hurling abuse if they were not.

The whole day was like a nightmare.

But mum gets home, it's been a hot day, she cools down and has a cup of tea.   In about half an hour the door opens and the boys come into the room. The boys begin to tell her how very sorry they are for giving her such a terrible day. They are both very contrite.

"Oh," I say, "so what did you say?"

"Well," she said, "I told them that I was SO pleased that they were prepared to apologise."

"What happened then?"

"We all had a really big cuddle," she told me happily.

On the face of it this mother is entitled to be pleased. Her boys have been abusive and tormented her all day—and here they come to tell her that they are really sorry for this. What could possibly be wrong with that? There is a lot that's wrong.

I asked the Mum, "Did the relief from tension for you and the boys and your mutual pleasure that you were friends again make this cuddle particularly heartfelt and warm?"

"Oh yes," she said.

"When," I asked her, "have you had a cuddle as intense and warm as that when your boys **had a really good day**?"

The answer, of course, was, "never."

If you, the parent, have done nothing wrong, then you should not be "making up." Making up has an intensity all of its own that is almost impossible to replicate when children have behaved well. If they had behaved well, not only would the cuddle have been less intense; it is unlikely to have happened at all.

For these boys the tunnel of bad behaviour that they entered at the start of the day now has clear light at the end. The next time they are tempted to enter it they will feel secure that the outcome will be OK, in fact there is a bonus: *"If we play our cards right we can have our mum even **more** loving and attentive because we have spent a whole day torturing her."*

How should you handle this apology then?
Of course you should accept apologies, but this acceptance
should always be provisional. Remind them that apologising is
meaningless if at the very next occasion they do not even
attempt to act differently. Rewards and praise should be used
carefully even for actual change in behaviour but especially for
throwaway statements of contrition.

These boys take the initiative to apologise—of course this is
positive, even if they are partly doing it manipulate.

This parent might have said, "Well I am pleased that you both
have come to apologise, however…."

You can make it clear that the apology does not reverse the
sanctions you have given, and that, although you are pleased,
what you really want is for them to strive harder to control the
behaviour next time.

So to recap, the 8 sanction-avoidance strategies are
1. **Saying "I don't care"**
2. **Saying "If you punish me I'll punish you"**
3. **Trying to tire you out / wear you down**
4. **Attempting to make you feel guilty**
   ("it's not fair" / "look how bad it makes me feel")
5. **Questioning what you said the rule really was**
6. **Lying—saying they didn't do it**
7. **Saying they will behave well now (if you don't
   impose the sanction)**
8. **Trying to charm or joke to undermine your
   seriousness**
9. **Expecting warmth from you too soon and under
   their terms**

<u>Remember, once applied, a sanction cannot be reversed.</u>
Remember, none of the child's ways of subverting our sanctions can work if firstly, we make sure we are acting fairly and warn our child **beforehand**, and secondly, if we **never** reverse the sanction once it has been applied, **whatever** the child says or does.

Chapter Seven

The Real World as a Template

Parents won't "spoil" the child.
We should always strive to give our children what they want.
We do not "spoil" our children by giving them things; this is a
complete fallacy. We can give our children all manner of things,
and as long as they are given under our terms, we will do our
children no harm whatever. What needs to be avoided at all
costs is giving the child something against our better judgement,
or after we have already said "no," or when they have been
nagging us, or when the way they ask suggests they will not
accept "no."

The real world
There is a simpler way to put this: Never, ever, give them what
they want for behaviour that would not work in the real world
outside your home. It is only if you break **this one rule** that you
"spoil" them; what you "spoil" is their chance of joining the real
world and being happy in it.

Parents have often become completely de-skilled by the
conflicting advice they have been given. Often the answers to
the broader issues that puzzle us can be found simply by
looking at what will need to happen in the real world outside the
home. We love our children, they remain our babies, and we
sometimes forget our prime directive—to fit them for the real
world. To see what I mean, have a look at this email sent to me
by a worried mother:

"Apart from always arguing and not wanting to do as he is told, I am becoming increasingly worried by my son's obsessive behaviour. He is six. He must have his socks at just the right height and when he is tucked in he has to have the bedclothes 'just so.' Sometimes I have to go back five times before he is satisfied. I am very worried what should I do."

This mother is worried by an alleged "obsession" of her son. But which world does she inhabit, her son's world—where you need to be tucked in five times—or the real world where you don't? **She is the one** who comes back five times rather than say it really isn't necessary. By doing this she places herself squarely in her son's non-logical world, and she cannot help him with his "obsession" while joining him in it.

Here is another example.

Rewarding Bad Behaviour

Look closely at what this parent says:

"Most situations at home are usually overcome with some sort of reward, i.e. a trip to MacDonald's, etc. School seems to be the main area for his bad behaviour. Perhaps this is because we have just learned to be extremely patient parents dealing with a wilful child and become used to his behaviour at home. We have always been firm with him and will not 'give in' to him."

It is not mentioned here, but the "situations" that this mother is talking about occur when her son threatens a temper tantrum if he does not get his own way. His behaviour is calmed once a reward is offered. Again, this mother needs to ask, where is her son going to find a world where disappointments come with an immediate compensatory reward whenever you make a big fuss? This mother may be saying the right things to her son, but the real lesson she is teaching is, *be rude—refuse—make a big fuss—and you get a reward.*

Parents like this mother think that when they offer the reward and the child stops the bad behaviour they are rewarding the child stopping, but the child cannot get this reward **unless he first starts** behaving badly. This is what the parent actually is rewarding. This is the fundamental difference that turns a reward into a bribe. A bribe is a reward delivered at the wrong time—i.e., when the child is **already** behaving badly. For this parent to offer a reward for what should be ordinary behaviour is already a bad idea but what is really crazy here is that **if this child had been behaving well** his mother would not even have thought of the reward. Parents may miss the significance of this; their children won't. Behave badly and you are rewarded for it. The child will soon learn to devise all manner of new negative behaviours for you to placate. Your reward may solve the immediate problem, but the frequency of the "bad" behaviour goes sky high.

Times When You Must Not Try to Make Your Child Feel Better

It is far easier to inadvertently reward bad behaviour than you might think. We do it

- whenever we try to make our children feel better when the reason for their feeling bad is their own "bad" behaviour

63

- whenever we try to make our children feel better when their way of showing us they are not feeling good is itself "bad" or unwanted behaviour (whining is an obvious example)

- whenever we "reset" our relationship ("make up" too soon), i.e., when the child is still being rude or still sulking or is glib or manipulative

All of this means we must constantly watch what we are really rewarding even when we are following professional advice.

A child psychologist explains to parents that it's advisable to put children in "time out" for the number of minutes that corresponds to their age. Thus four minutes if the child is four years old and five minutes if the child is five, and so on. This advice is presumably designed to prevent young children being put in isolation for too long. But since time, not behaviour, dictates when the child is allowed to leave, it is entirely possible that when the parent goes to get the child out the child will have begun screaming in temper in an attempt to force their parents to let them out. The child will assume that angry rather than calm behaviour is the reason for his or her release. This "time out" ends at the wrong time and rewards the wrong behaviour. The ferocity of the tantrum behaviour will probably get worse because the ending of the "time out" is rewarding an increase in the very behaviour it was intend to change.

Chapter Eight

No child repeats ineffective behaviour, so if you continue to get temper tantrums after the "toddler" stage, your child must be getting something from them. Parents reward the child for having the tantrum. The first reward is the way a tantrum concentrates the parents' attention and focuses it on the child. This is why so many behaviour specialists recommend that parents ignore bad behaviour. Unfortunately, completely ignoring a tantrum is often not an option, as it tempts the child to do something that cannot be ignored. The second way in which parents often reward the tantrum is by allowing themselves to be worn down or intimidated, and they "give in" in some way. Children become "hooked" on the reward of attention, and also take the opportunity to return any anger and frustration that parents have shown to them. Mercury's child is rarely happy.

If children only continue to have tantrums if they work, if they are rewarded, then there is only one cure for tantrums. Parents who come to me so desperately want there to be another answer. There is no other answer, there is only the one answer. **You cannot get rid of a behaviour that you consistently reward**. The only strategy that works is to have sympathy for the how the child is feeling, but to consistently sanction the behaviour that the child uses to **express** the feelings—**never** giving in to the intimidation. Children have a right to say how they feel, but do not have a right to **demonstrate** how they feel.

If parents don't manage to minimise the rewards the child gets, then tantrums can continue well into the teenage years and beyond. The longer you allow temper tantrums to work, the more extreme they tend to get, and the more the tantrum will escalate when you attempt to stand firm. However difficult it may be to stand up to a tantrum today, parents need to remember that in a year's time their child will be a year bigger and a year more determined.

A scary fact—an accident waiting to happen
Regardless of your child's threats, **at some point, there will be issues that you cannot concede**. Eventually, what Mercury's child will ask for will be more dangerous than the behaviour he or she threatens you with if you do not concede. In the worst case, when this happens, your child will have had no practice in losing these confrontations and you will have no practice in staying firm. If you give in to temper tantrums, your home becomes an accident waiting to happen.

The difference between a demand and a request is straightforward: A request accepts two possible outcomes, a demand only one. Often the demand becomes so usual that it becomes the child's only way of asking and parents become used to it. What we no longer see we cannot change. A child who asks in a way that suggests he or she will **not accept** the "wrong" answer is demanding, not asking.

When my daughter was around eight years old she asked me if she could go and play with her friends across the road, and, as was usually the case, I said that she could. She misheard me and thought I had said that she couldn't go. Upset and angry, she said,

"That's not fair! You always let me go to play with them! Why can't I play with them today? They will be expecting me!"

I had said that she could go and she had misunderstood, but now she was demanding to go. I said,

*"Nadia, you asked me if you could go and I said yes, but you misheard me and thought that I said no. But now you are acting as if I don't have **the right** to say you can't go. So now you really can't go."*

This rule is vital for children—demands must never work.

The Tantrum—The Ultimate Demand

1. **Sympathetic tone**

    You will not give in, but when you need to speak to your child, use a sympathetic tone even though he or she is angry. Remember your child is often completely trapped by this behaviour. Make sure your voice and actions show no anger, but let him know what the consequences are for each act of rudeness or aggressive behaviour. Do not agree even to reasonable requests that are made rudely or aggressively.

2. **Life goes on**

    You will not give in, but concentrate on keeping your

face and voice calm. Go on about your usual activity—invent an activity if necessary (walk past the child to get some towels out of the cupboard or to put something away)—so that you give the impression that in spite of all the noise and confusion you are not fazed. A good ploy can be to shout to your partner with some everyday request, "John, would you programme 'East Enders' on the video for me please?" Show your child that "life goes on."

3. No concessions

NO CONCESSIONS. Your child may well be having the tantrum because he or she has had a disappointment, or they may be trying to get you to reverse a decision you have made. Lean over backwards to be fair in the first place, but NEVER placate or make concessions once a temper tantrum is signalled or has actually begun. You will merely be solving this tantrum at the cost of many more in the future.

4. If you can possibly avoid it, try your hardest NOT to, hold restrain, force or carry your child

This is not always possible, but you should try to avoid physical contact with your child during a tantrum. If you do have to do it, then always warn your child first, giving him or her a chance to comply and avoid coercion. The reason for this is that Mercury's child often finds touching in the middle of a tantrum rewarding (even aggressive touching and hitting). This becomes **truer** as interactions in the home deteriorate and the more positive touching stops.

5. Never be intimidated into NOT sanctioning your child's behaviour

The power and violence of the temper tantrum will just become more and more serious if you are intimidated and avoid using sanctions. Your priority in the past may have been to stop the tantrum at all costs. **This is the wrong goal**—this is the reason your child is still having tantrums. Whether the child stops the tantrum or not, the issue that has created the tantrum must NEVER be conceded to the child. Your goal should be to stop the tantrum only after

- not giving in to the demands
- providing consequences for each shouted rudeness or broken item or hit or kick he gives

A small (non-angry, reluctantly given) sanction for each action that you feel you cannot ignore (throwing, breaking, tearing, hitting) may actually **increase** the length or intensity of the current tantrum but will decrease the frequency of tantrums in general.

In summary, be sympathetic, warn before you sanction, implement the sanction with reluctance, and encourage your child to avoid more sanctions—but NEVER avoid giving consequences for your child's unacceptable actions. (Obviously, safety can be a reason to break this rule—but perhaps even then at the cost of greater long-term danger.)

Chapter Nine

The Seven C's Positive Sanction Method

If parents want their sanctions (punishments) to be effective, there are seven things they need to remember. Some mistakes when sanctioning are easily missed.

Parents must take the time to read **all of this book** carefully before they attempt to use these seven rules. The seven C's method is very powerful and very effective, but will not work by itself if you have not understood the principles behind the method. My clients get daily support and advice with their sanction system, but you will have to work out for yourself where you may be going wrong; so read the preceding and succeeding chapters carefully.

Remember, your child has probably been manipulating and controlling your responses to his/her behaviour for many months or years and is probably an expert at undermining your resolve. **Don't think** that once you have begun to use this method that they will immediately stop being rude or immediately comply with your wishes. They won't. Nevertheless, if you don't get discouraged and if you consistently provide the consequences for their behaviour without the old rewards of your anger and attention, **this will stop and they will comply.**

If you are lucky, and many are, change will begin to happen within a week or two. For others it can be much longer.

However, ask yourself this: "What alternative is there to my modelling the control that I want my child to display and consistently and relentlessly providing sanctions for EACH of his or her rude and hurtful statements or actions?"

Remember, I have not, to date, had a failure with this system with any of my clients who stuck to it, so if it does not appear to be working, try to work out which of the rules you may be breaking.

If any one of the seven stages is missing, your sanctions will not be effective.

So let's go. Take your time to absorb each rule:

The Seven C's

---

1. Catch

Concentrate so you catch your child being (even a little) rude or delaying or refusing.
In a pleasant way correct your child for **everything** that is not completely acceptable.

2. Calm and clear

State (re-state) what you want in a friendly and calm way, even if you KNOW your child will respond by refusing rudely. You do not need anger for emphasis to make it clear you are being categorical, your Caution (next) will do that for you.

3. Caution   Make sure your friendly words don't give a choice or suggest that you have not really made up your mind, i.e., don't say, "I think you ought to come in now."

4. Cut-off point   If your child does not comply, then caution (warn) your child that you don't want to have to use "X" where "X" is the precise—and small and repeatable—consequence you have decided upon.

5. Choice   State the precise point at which it will be too late for your child to comply: "Come on John, if you haven't gotten your trousers on by the time I come back downstairs, you will lose...."

6. Consequence   Your child chooses **to do** what you have asked, or chooses **to ignore** the cut-off-point.

If your child has chosen to do what you have asked, go immediately back to being relaxed and OK. Say

NOTHING. Don't gloat about your victory—say NOTHING about the fact that they have not done what you asked immediately (or any other sting in the tale remark). It is YOUR system and they have succeeded within it—so be completely satisfied

or,

if your child has chosen **to ignore** the cut-off point, then without anger tell your child that the sanction has now been applied. Again say NOTHING more, or else you will give the impression that you have a problem with their choice or— more important— that you do not think your own sanction is sufficient. Your job is to provide consequences and you have done your job—let the sanction do the work. Your child DOES NOT have to comply here and now for the sanction to work.

If you are NOT silent (and talk outside the seven C's method), this is the point where you will slip back to your old "battle of wills" approach, and your child will not even notice that you have sanctioned him or her, and will find it easier to defy you.

7. **Cut all (non-seven C's) talk on behaviour**

"Yes but my child **will** argue!" Don't be fazed—this is almost guaranteed to happen at first. If your child argues about being sanctioned, don't be drawn in, or you will give the impression that the sanction is open to discussion. Rather, treat the argument as a NEW behaviour. In other words, if your child is rude or loud, quietly go back to ONE (Catch it) above, and move again through the seven C's. You must make sure that the child's objection to being sanctioned does not prevent it from happening, and make sure that the child's objecting just brings on **another** sanction. Gradually, in time, (if you follow all the seven C's), he will stop objecting.

Say NOTHING at any time about your child's behaviour except the **minimum** required while carrying out the seven C's method.

You may not be convinced that this aspect of your previous method was counter-productive. **But it was.** This is vital—if you cannot stop yourself from doing this, your child's behaviour **will not change.**

Let the Sanction Do the Work

An old craftsman I knew as a boy was a kind old man who used to let me and my brother use the tools in his workshop. One day, when I was sawing a piece of wood, he looked down at me and said,

"Son, what are you doing?"

I said, "I'm sawing this piece of wood."

"Yes," he said, "you are, aren't you...but you shouldn't be…that's the saw's job. Let the saw do the work.."

I looked at him, puzzled. He took the saw from my hands and explained that it had very sharp teeth and weight of its own, and it did not need to be pushed downwards. "Just draw it across the wood and let it do the work for you—let the saw do the work.."

Parents so often try too hard to change their children's behaviour when they should be staying calm and letting **"the sanction do the work."**

It's not the parents' job **to change their child's behaviour**.
Parents are always astonished when I say this. Of course, if you
train your child to accept consequences your child's behaviour
will change, but it is not your job to make those changes happen
right there and then when each problem occurs. It is entirely
your child's job. Your job is much simpler. Your job is to
provide the consequences—the sanctions—and let those do the
work for you. The more you try to change your children's
behaviour through your strength of will, the less effective you
will be. Whether your child follows your instruction or not, you
should try not to show too much concern either way. Let the
sanction do the work. Your job is to make sure that the
consequences you specify inexorably follow the choice your
child makes. Do not be so determined to get your own way right
away, or you will use up the sanctions that you will need later.

Chapter Ten

Rewards

Rewarding a Mercurian child for "good" behaviour in the home gives entirely the wrong message. If we reward ordinary polite behaviour, it tells children that this is something exceptional and that each time they produce it they should get something for it. Children can be rewarded for the effort that they **put in** to change their behaviour, but this distinction is not always easy to make.

Children sometimes see changing for the better as "backing down." Providing a reward or making comments like, "you see, it wasn't so bad was it?" or even praising the child on these occasions is the last thing a wise parent does. Too much notice of change can be experienced as a punishment, because Mercury's child is quite capable of being punished by something we intend to be a reward. They are also capable of being rewarded by something that we intend to be a punishment, and this is the underlying reason why an alternative to the endless round of discussion and "telling off" has to be found. The talk, the attention, and the "telling off" function just like a reward in most households.

It is best if parents stay completely away from **dedicated rewards.** When we say, *"If you are well behaved in the shop I will get you an ice-cream on the way home,"* we take all responsibility from the child. We are actually training the child that what **should be** ordinary everyday behaviour is exceptional. We are effectively giving a bribe. How can we promise the child something **this time** and expect the child to behave well for nothing **next time?**

The difference between a bribe and a reward is in the timing.

<u>Nothing is for nothing</u>
If you want to use the ice-cream as an incentive, then we need to have it in place as part **of the routine** for the trip back home. Although rewards for *this* and for *that* are a very bad idea, a highly rewarding climate is not. If you have first made your home routine as rewarding as possible, it is relatively easy to train your child that everything he or she finds rewarding is contingent upon reasonable behaviour. In other words, the ice-cream can be withdrawn. Mercury's child needs **at all times** to have rewarding events or interactions anticipated. The child is rewarded just for being him or her (if the child is being reasonable, of course), **rather than** for specific "good" behaviour.

A Reward-Rich Home

We do not "spoil" our children by making home as rewarding as possible. Without a rewarding environment, it becomes almost impossible to devise effective sanctions. The sanctions we use should consist of the incremental withdrawal of naturally occurring rewards. Nothing rewarding, apart from our love, should be provided regardless of behaviour. In the home, as in life, nothing is for nothing. This means we need to control naturally occurring rewards; no child that has a problem with behaviour should be able to reward him- or herself.

Some years ago I went to an icy tower block in London to speak to parents who had asked for help. The family was experiencing serious behaviour problems. I arrived in the midst of a crisis. Two hours earlier, the boy, an 11-year-old, had refused to go to school, abused his parents, kicked his mother, broken a table lamp and left the flat, slamming the door. As we were talking, a cold draught of air told us that the boy had returned. We halted our conversation and waited, and we heard a cupboard open in the kitchen. In a few moments the boy appeared still wearing his anorak, and he stood, leaning on the doorframe, eating a Mars Bar.

This boy behaves in this way because he has learnt that he does not need to care about the outcomes for this type of behaviour. Before he left, this boy refused to go to school, abused his parents, kicked his mother, knocked the table lamp onto the floor, and slammed the front door—he has now returned, and the first thing he was able to do was **reward himself** with chocolate. This family's behaviour problem is so serious and this boy's future is in so much danger that his ability to reward himself at the wrong times should not be possible. All access to rewarding activities in this house should be contingent on his behaviour and be in the control of his parents. Once he begins to accept his parents' right to use these natural rewards, the cost to him will be minimal. If his parents are clever, they will **increase** the good things just before they begin to use them to encourage his better behaviour. Mercury's child is an outsider in his own home. He controls the home without feeling part of it. All the good things in this boy's home are considered his **right**, but his parents should have the ability to ask that when the view from his Mercurian world collides with the view from theirs—

politeness, bedtime, homework, going to school, etc.—he realises that only earth values provide natural rewards.

Nothing to lose

Home has to remain a rewarding place in spite of **anything and everything** that the child does. We must not run out of sanctions, so the child must not run out of rewards. This means that if we get angry we cannot take away this reward and that reward like there is no tomorrow. Distraught clients often begin by telling me that they have taken virtually everything away from the child as punishments. When parents do this, we put ourselves in the worst possible position. We make the child **even more angry** and uncooperative while at the same time arranging that the child has **nothing to lose**. No rewards mean no sanctions. You must never run out of natural rewards. To run out of rewards is also to run out of consequences. If we run out, use them all up, we become powerless.

A Crazy-Sounding Mantra

Parents must never run out of sanctions, hence this crazy-sounding mantra:

The worse the behaviour and the more frequently it occurs, the **smaller (the more repeatable / sustainable)** *the sanction* **(the withdrawal of reward)** *needs to be.*

Chapter Eleven

Your Child's Need for Attention

Preserving your pre-child self

All your efforts to stop your child from getting attention in the wrong way will be for nothing if you do not give your time freely when your child is behaving normally. Sometimes parents have told me that they vowed when they had children they would still have a life of their own. This is fine, but as a client of mine discovered, we need to be careful not to take this too far. A family I had just started working with had gone on holiday, and the mother phoned me to say that their second day had been terrible:

"It was my turn to have some free time and it was Michael's (her husband's) turn to keep the children (twin boys of six) happy. It was a nightmare. I was trying to read on the beach and the boys kept interrupting me for increasingly ridiculous reasons. I had a terrible afternoon."

I had to explain the way these interactions work—the more freely you give attention to children, the less they need. The more you push them away, the more frantically they fight for your attention, and the quicker they hit on the failsafe method of achieving it—bad behaviour. The next day she showed interest and responded to everything they said and was amazed how quickly they began to leave her and play on their own without needing her attention.

Not personality

Most of the parents I have worked with over the years have been convinced that their children were strong-willed, defiant, selfish personalities, but it always turned out that their behaviour was not caused by personality at all. Behaviour that in every case changed within a few weeks could not have been caused by personality.

The Child Can Think or Say ANYTHING

In the preface to this book we said that this was not a *"back-to-basics"* book, and that *"the main purpose of this book is to encourage parents to analyse and avoid all polarised views of parenting."*

This desire to avoid an extreme view is not new; if you take an historical look at the changes in child-rearing advice, you will discover that it has always had a balance. Earlier writers, even the Victorians, were far less scary and draconian than some current writers on behaviour who appear to have views that are a throw-back to a time that never existed. Look at this "Victorian" article from
The Times:

*The father, **whose baby had died from her injuries**, claimed to have been feeding her using an "authoritative" technique recently taught to him by hospital staff. The method involved holding her head gently so that she could not move it, saying "no" while looking into her eyes and reintroducing the bottle to her mouth..*

The word "no" is meaningless to the baby. It is just a loud sound that startles it and may make it relax its mouth for a second. Whilst it might be argued that a dispassionate nurse in a hospital could carry out this procedure, keep it within acceptable limits, and not persist if it is not working, it is difficult to see how ordinary tired, distraught, and sometimes traumatised parents could be expected to. It is difficult not to wonder how this differs from a description of "forced feeding." What is really worrying is this is not really a Victorian account. I copied it word-for-word from *The Times* in 2004.

What are children allowed to do?
It has always been thought important to have a clear idea about what the child **is** allowed to do. Mercury's child, any child, has the right to think and speak freely. Mercury's child is entitled to his or her view and is entitled to express it. There are only two limitations:
He or she is

not allowed to express their view rudely or aggressively

and,

not allowed, however politely, to go on and on restating their view once a decision has been made.

No system that prevents children from expressing themselves will work. A child really can say, and should be encouraged to say, **anything**—provided it is not expressed rudely. The best way to illustrate this is to take the expletive "fuck off." No parent is happy when their child tells them to "fuck off," but the content of this expression is acceptable. "Fuck off" is an obscene way of saying "go away," with these particular words chosen to express the child's anger. What if a child said to his or her mother in a calm, non-condescending voice,

"Mum, I'm feeling very angry with you at the moment. Could you give some time to myself, please?"

Most parents would be happy to comply. Mercury's child should not be encouraged to **not say** what they are thinking, but should be trained **how to say** what they are thinking. **Children can say anything**.

The Child Is Entitled to a Predicted Future

I am ten years old and I am engrossed in a story on children's television when my father comes in. He takes off his coat and retrieves his cigarettes from the pocket, then looks in the packet and says to me,

"Son, go down to the corner shop and get me some cigarettes, please."

It is difficult to describe how hurt and angry this made me feel. It was more than just the loss of a story in which I was engrossed. Why should such an ordinary request make a child so angry? The answer is that anyone who has predicted their future for the next couple of hours and has that expectation suddenly changed tends, unless it is a pleasant surprise, to be irritated. This lack of being able to predict happens far more to children than it does to adults, and far more in some families than it does in others. If my father came it at a set time and asked me to get his cigarettes in the middle of my children's programmes every single day I would, once I got used to it, not get so angry. Children need to be able to predict their immediate future. They need to be warned of changes or reminded when they are engrossed that the fun will end in ten minutes. The mother with the new baby who constantly tells an older child,

"Oh Jennifer, just pass me the …."

will get a far more negative reaction than if Jennifer had a defined set of chores that she did each day. Or if it was her job to help with the changing **every** time.

Chapter Twelve

Bedtime

I am at my wits' end with my daughter. She flatly refuses to do anything I say most of the time and although I feel I can cope with it during the day (just!), bedtime has become a real battle. She just refuses to stay in her bed or even her room once I have said goodnight. I have tried allsorts—reasoning with her, bribery, depriving her of things, yelling (loudly), even ignoring her. None of it works. Bedtime is usually around 8.30 but despite a calm routine it can be 10.30 (on a good night) or midnight before she is asleep. She is not tired the following morning but becomes grumpy during the day. Although she is VERY active she just doesn't seem to run out of steam! My husband works away a lot so I often have to deal with this on my own. I work part time and am really glad to go to work some days just to escape the battles! I am desperate to get her to go to bed without any fuss or arguing and for her to stay in bed and go to sleep at a reasonable hour. Any advice you could give me I would really appreciate. P.S. My other daughter sleeps well and usually goes to bed without a fuss.

More parents reward the **wrong** behaviour at bedtime than at any other time. The child gets out of bed and often leaves his or her room, and we give them lots of attention in our attempt to get them back to bed.

Bedtime is hard for children. They are left on their own, often for the only time in the whole day, and they feel lonely and neglected. The child calls or gets out of bed and their problem is solved—the only cost being the increasing irritation coming from their parents. For Mercury's child this is always a price worth paying. If it is negative attention versus no attention, then it is no contest. Each time the child calls or comes out of the room the reward (the attention) is given to him or her. The child is rewarded because he or she has **stopped** trying to sleep. Parents reward children if they **stop trying**. This is one of the easiest behaviours to control if we make sure we reward the child for trying to sleep and **not** for getting up.

Sleep mode
The child has his or her eyes shut, body still and relaxed, with no talking or fidgeting. Since we cannot ask him or her to actually fall asleep, the child is doing everything we want. All we can ask is that they stay in "sleep mode" and, if they do, this is worth rewarding with our attention. So we sit next to a child that is in sleep mode and reward the behaviour with our presence. We whisper that we will have to go if the child tries to speak to us or opens their eyes or fidgets. If they do these things we say that we will go but come back if they stop doing these things. We gradually train our child not to need us in the room. We will tell them we will be back in a second and quietly slip outside the door, count to five and come back, usually to find that the child has sat up in bed or is trying to get out of it to follow us. We whisper that we cannot come into the room because they are not in "sleep mode" or, for the younger ones, not in "sleepy time." Immediately they settle down and we come back in to reward them. We continue to train them to accept our longer absences with our assurance that **we will come back**.

Nothing demonstrates the power of getting the reward in the right place than this technique. Most children can be trained to stay in bed with a minimal amount of support within two weeks.

The Problem to Tackle First

This is the problem we need to tackle first. Of all the problems that parents have with their children sleep problems are the most serious. Lack of adequate sleep is by far the most common cause of angry behaviour and tantrums during the day. What is a reasonable bedtime? Mercury's child has hit upon a classic way of undermining parental resolve. The child tells the parents that everybody else's parents, bar none, let their children go to bed far later than this child.

I am always amazed how many parents fall for this. When you ask them how many parents that **they know** that have a later bedtime, they are usually hard put to tell you.

Much more sleep
It is rare for children with behaviour problems to be getting anywhere near the amount of sleep that they need. Our children's need for sleep comes before their need for almost any thing else. Certainly before after school clubs and evening phone calls to their friends. There is, in my view, nowhere near as much difference between the sleep needs of an eight-year-old and a fourteen-year-old as parents think. An ideal time for a fourteen year-old would be around 8.30 p.m., which is a time from which most would sleep the full night. The absolute latest should around 9.30 p.m.

For younger children the ideal time for bed is often impossible, since getting home from school and having a meal and taking a bath take the child past that time. The absolute latest for a child of five would be 7 p.m.

Gradually Reduce Bedtime

A child that is going to bed an hour later than he or she should will not be able to sleep if the time is suddenly reduced. If parents organise well they can do everything five minutes earlier each evening. Children can usually cope with a gradual change, and often younger ones do not even realise the time is changing. In just twelve days, using this method, the child will be going to sleep an hour earlier.

Older children may have not ever accepted our right to specify a bedtime, and they will be unwilling to change. In the end the best way to support the change is to leave it completely to your child and say nothing other than the amount of pocket money or Game Boy time you will deduct for each minute past bedtime. Remember, it is not your job to change the behaviour, just to make sure that consequences are not avoided.

Chapter Thirteen

Start Day

Parents now need to choose a day to start the new regime. It may be best to explain to the children what will now be happening in the evening and start the system the next morning. The new system needs to be applied to all of the children in the family equally, not just the child parents are more concerned about. It may be that parents do not feel the others need it but if they introduce it just for one child it will fail immediately—as we said earlier, it will just become another statement of dissatisfaction, another indication of the targeted child's difference. The other children are probably just as much in need of change; parents are often so focused on the extreme behaviour of a particular child that they do not realise how poorly their other children behave.

Parents may well have tried and discarded much advice and many strategies in the past; much of what was discarded may well have been necessary for any change to occur but not sufficient by itself to produce the change. For this reason parents should not knowingly introduce their own version of what they have read here. If any parent still does not know what the difference is between a sanction and an "interpersonal sanction," then please go back and find out. This is a crucial distinction. With just one missing element from any of the rules and guidelines in this book, the house of cards will fall.

<u>Start Day</u>
Explain to your child or children the way things will now be for **all of you**. Explain the positive aspects of the new regime. Explain what they will be getting each day in fruit or sweets or chocolate or cake and/or T.V. time, computer time, pocket money, and so on.

Sometimes a targeted child may assume that the changes are being made because that child is "bad"; make sure that he or she is clear this is not so. Usually, if you sell the positive aspects, they will listen. Should they give you a hard time, just start using the system and let them see how it works in practice. Stay calm, don't get angry. The most common response is interest with a little scepticism. Occasionally parents get a downright putdown with laughter. If this is what happens, smile along with them—what they think at the beginning has no influence on the outcome.

Don't allow them to suggest any modifications to the system. They will usually make suggestions that remove some of the negative effects on them, and in any case it is your system, not theirs. You are **not** asking them if they want to try the new system; you are informing them about what will happen.

Once you start, remember that before your children come into a room or you go into one you must think, "Mode." Not what they say, but the way they say it. It is their **mode of speaking** that you are interested in. Say, "That sounds a little rude, Jamie," and only start mentioning sanctions if Jamie starts arguing about, or not accepting, the training:

"Come on, Jamie. I don't want to have to take a 5 pence from your pocket money."

Keep School and Home Separate

Remember to keep school and home separate. If the child has had a bad day at school, try to let the school sanction the behaviour. If you have to sanction children for their behaviour at school, have a set, small, consequence ready that they know about in advance. Try to find a sanction that can happen automatically without putting the child in your bad books before the evening has even started.

Chapter Fourteen

In general the main theoretical approaches to behaviour change are:

1. **Behavioural:** Problems due to maladaptive learning; uses rewards and punishments

2. **Person-centred:** Problems due to child's self-concept; aims to redress discrepancies between the child's actual and ideal self

3. **Cognitive behavioural:** Problems due to maladaptive thinking; uses training for erroneous or unrealistic thinking

4. **Psychodynamic:** Problems due to unresolved unconscious conflicts; helps child to gain insight and increase ego strength

THIS APPROACH
This approach believes that chronic bad behaviour creates what we have termed an "interactive behaviour imbalance" (www.ibi.org.uk). It does not see "bad behaviour" as the child's problem at all, but rather an interactional problem between child and parent, which the child is incapable of changing. The System or Intervention therefore works exclusively through parents, through their perceptions of what is happening.

Theoretical position
The principles that form the basis of the I.B.I change system.

The I.B.I. approach is mainly behavioural.
There are four reasons why, in this view, the behavioural approach is the best-suited for use with children who are badly behaved. The behavioural approach

1. Does not require the child to have reached any particular level of conceptual development.

2. Enables the parents to remain as the "agents of change." This means that they can make changes without a loss of leadership or the child being made too aware that an outside agency is involved.

3. The parents can then be trained to change their own behaviour and to focus on the interactive nature of the problem.

4. All parents already use an intuitive version of the behavioural approach—they use rewards and punishments instinctively. However, lack of precision in their use is always, in Warwick's view, one of the main reasons for the problems parents experience. Warwick has found it essential to train parents to use rewards and sanctions effectively.

Influences of the other approaches:
Person-centred
Although he works exclusively with parents Warwick sees the child's perception of what the parents think of him/her as central. Through exclusively behavioural methods, he trains parents to maintain a positive approach and reduce discrepancies between how the child would like to view him or herself and the view they see reflected from their parents.

Cognitive behavioural
An intuitive version of this third view is also often found in use
by parents. They are very often engaged in continuous attempts
to change what their children appear to think. This often just
adds to the problems, and parents need clear strategies to avoid
this trap. When working with badly behaved children, Warwick
does not view their apparent maladaptive, erroneous, or
unrealistic processing as a problem associated with thinking at
all, but rather one generated by a lack of training to accept
consequences.

He believes problems stem from an emotional need to suspend
logic rather than a lack of logical thinking ability. He finds that
the unhelpful or unrealistic ways that children appear to think
are effectively changed by careful use of a combination of
techniques linking rewards and sanctions consistently and
positively applied.

The problem with many behaviour interventions
Warwick believes that taking too little account of the interactive
nature of "bad behaviour" handicaps many interventions. "Bad
behaviour" is always, in his view, part of an interactional
problem.

Warwick believes that it is vital for professionals not to work
too far away from these interactions. For him, the parents'
response to behaviour is always the key factor. He believes
professionals need to put themselves on the line and suffer
constant feedback from the results of their advice.

Don't blame parents
This system maintains that it makes no sense to blame parents
for the bad behaviour of their children. The vast majority have

always done their best and have often found it difficult to find effective help.

The need for research
The following conclusions are all intuitively based but present some interesting and concise areas for future research:

Position on behaviour disorders
When is "bad" behaviour "serious"? When does a child's behaviour warrant being described as a "disorder"? Perhaps the only honest answer is at the point when the skill of the parents and the professionals advising them runs out.

I.B.I. work suggests that, since many diagnoses of behaviour disorders do not come with any comprehensive advice on behaviour management, it is probably best to assume, unless the professionals specifically say otherwise, that the techniques that work with "chronic bad behaviour" will still be needed. Although there is currently no research to back it up, I.B.I. work inclines some to the belief that many behaviour disorders merely predispose the child and the parent to have problems interacting rather than making it inevitable that the child will behave badly. Interactive behaviour techniques may not alter the underlying behaviour disorder (ADHD, for instance), but may dramatically change the trauma of living with it.

Common characteristics
Although, again, research is needed to confirm his observations, Warwick believes that children with "chronic bad behaviour" have a range of characteristics as predictable as those associated with the recognised behaviour disorders. He has introduced the concept of "interactive behaviour imbalance" not to create another behaviour disorder but to show that "bad behaviour" is

always a problem shared by the child and the parent. It is, therefore, essential to search for both the problem and the solution within these "interactions".

<u>Characteristics of the child with "Interactive Behaviour Imbalance"</u>
I.B.I. method involves speaking to clients every day, including weekends, until the behaviour problem is solved. Working in this way has produced some remarkable insights. By far the most interesting is the realisation that I.B.I. or badly behaved children have remarkably similar characteristics. (**See Chapter Three.**)

Appendix

I'm after some help with my **2 year old son** who is extremely active and hits me and always says No! Never can I make him happy. He appears to be compulsive, nags for hours over anything. Won't share anything. It's his way or no way. Am I in the right place coming to you or is this normal two-year-old behaviour?

I am at my wits end with my youngest daughter aged **3.5 yrs**. She flatly refuses to do anything I say most of the time and although feel I can cope with it during the day (just!), bedtime has become a real battle. She just refuses to stay in her bed or even her room once I have said goodnight. I have tried allsorts—reasoning with her, bribery, depriving her of things, yelling (loudly) even ignoring her. None of it works. Bedtime is usually around 7.30 but despite a calm routine it can be 9.30 (on a good night) or midnight before she is asleep. She is not tired the following morning but becomes grumpy during the day. Although she is VERY active she just doesn't seem to run out of steam! My husband works away a lot so I often have to deal with this on my own. I work part

103

time and am really glad to go to work some days just to escape the battles!

I am desperate to get her to go to bed without any fuss or arguing and for her to stay in bed and go to sleep at a reasonable hour. Any advice you could give me I would really appreciate. P.S. My other daughter aged nearly 6 sleeps well and usually goes to bed without a fuss.

I am having a problem with my **4 year old** being very rude and sarcastic towards not only us but his sister and other family members. It seems to mostly happen when he is not getting what he wants, he is very impatient when things don't go his way. My husband and I have tried teaching him that if you are patient that maybe it will work out but this doesn't seem to work. For example on his rudeness, every time I tell him what we are having for supper he reponds with "I'M NOT EATING THAT" and then starts with "fine then, I won't eat." Now it is not just what he is saying but the manner in which it is said. He also cannot control his anger and usually lashes out not physically but verbally with many "I hate you's" and "you're not my friend." We have a 10 year old daughter and never encountered this problem with her therefore we are running out of ideas. If you have any suggestions

---

I hope you can help me. I have a **five year old son** (Jake) who is very strong-willed and challenging. I have tried several different methods of helping him with his behavior and nothing seems to be working. He recently started Kindergarten and just today, I received a call from his teacher saying that he had been in time-out twice. He gets very angry and screams, throws things, etc. He has an older brother who is eight. Ty is the most laid back, easygoing child. Jake has me exhausted daily and most days to the brink of tears. When asked to do a task, he will only do it if he wants to. If not, there is no "making him" do something. I am learning this only makes it worse. We have tried time-outs, taking things away and even a spanking. nothing fazes him. HELP!!!!! Thank you.

My **6 year old** has now been kicked out of two day care centers, she when told to sit in time out for something she might have done, rebels by hitting the teacher, and screaming and hitting the other kids. She will not or does not get along with other children, unless they play and do what she says. We've tried everything, from time out in her room, taking toys from her, taking certain privileges from her. Nothing at all works, I'm pulling my hair out. There are no babysitters that will watch her. What do I do for punishment?

I have a **seven year old daughter** who his having problems in school. The teacher sends her to the office for being disruptive in the classroom. She interrupts the teacher and when told to stop, she continues. She distracts the other kids in the same manner and becomes defiant when told to stop. At home she is somewhat the same, but we distract her either by reading books, printing, colouring or watching a movie. At school she has to follow their curriculum and there is no other way they say they can stop this other than sending her out of the classroom.

The PROBLEM: I come to my **eight year old's** behaviour now. He is very intelligent and I have devoted my time exclusively to him, reading to him, playing with him and engaging him in different activities. In the past 2-3 months, he has become

1. aggressive - he hits me, bangs into me in passing, punches me (supposedly in fun) and so on;

2. very loud - he is constantly yelling and testing my patience with this;

3. rude and cheeky - disrespectful and very rude (mostly with me)

When listed out like this, it may not seem very serious, but I am worried.

When I reprimand him/send him to his room for a 5 minute time-out/ask him to do anything (brush teeth/change clothes/get into bed/wash hands), he gets aggressive;

loud; angry and sometimes says hurtful things like "I don't like you!", etc., which really worries me.

I have an **9 year old** son who is rebelling against me and my new partner. Everything I do is not enough. I have tried to deprive him of his toys, food friends and anything else I can think of. I'm beaten and I hope you can help. He has taken to stealing what ever I will not provide for him. He will not do anything that is asked of him. CAN YOU PLEASE HELP?

My **9 and 10 year old daughters** have a love hate relationship going that at times truly challenges the serenity of my family. The 8 year old makes great grades in school, unless she is in a bad mood and then she doesn't do as well. Her 9 year old sister loves the world, sings constantly and is the definition of the compliant child. The 8 year old constantly compares her every action to her sister's, although we try to tell her that she does not have to compete with her sister and we are not comparing them. The 8 year old daughter awakes in the morning unhappy with the world at least 50% of the time, occasionally in a happy mood. She is quick to be angry at her sister in the AM if the sister's mood is too good. I realize there are a tremendous number of factors that affect each of us. I look forward to your advice and experience in this area.

My child is **10 years old** and is spoiled rotten. His father and I are divorced. I have custody. I have no help from his father on disciplining him. When I try to get him to clean his room, he tells me no he doesn't have to. He back talks me all the time and when he doesn't get his way he screams and throws things. I have grounded him, spanked him, took away his spending privileges, but nothing seems to work. I desperately need some advice.

Is it possible to have a talk with you about our son's problems? **He is 11**, a super-high achiever: gifted musician, sports record breaker, academic) etc. - unkind to his sister since she was born (he was 2 1/2 then) and now friendless, doubtless as a result of his over-bearing manner - (which he just cannot see). Parenting him is like working with a politician - I am a psychologist and it may be that I have reasoned too much with him....On the other hand he is loving, intelligent, humorous and a joy (when he's in a good mood). He feels so isolated at the moment and has such anger inside - punching holes in walls etc. - I am considering asking his school for help but am worried we will just get a label and no way forward.

My girlfriend and I are having tremendous problems with her **12 year old daughter** who throws really nasty tantrums then cannot remember why she has done this it is destroying our relationship. Her natural father has the same problems which lead to the marital split, he will only have her one night every two weeks because he can't cope. My own children do not like staying with us because of her behaviour. My girlfriend has had specialist help for her daughter without success can you help?

My son is 13 and having trouble adjusting to several changes: new home; new man in our life who is very demanding and pretty hard on him; new baby. His grades have dropped, he has trouble sleeping, he continues to ignore rules and requests, he has low self esteem, and has already tried smoking. He was an A/B honour student during first quarter of school. Second quarter he got a couple of D's and C's. Help!

One minute **my fourteen year old** son is the sweetest, most compassionate, loving child, and then the next he is verbally abusive and at times physically aggressive towards others (mainly his mother and sister). Every day seems to become an even bigger struggle to try and get him to be respectful, attentive, and get him to conduct himself appropriately. As a friend, I would like for you to send any information that you think may help us deal with our "unruly" child.

We have a **15 year old** son who has decided that he would like us to stay completely out of his life. Until the age of 13 he had extremely good grades, was tested as gifted in grade 4. We have tried to encourage him all the way along and made sure that he was participating in things he wanted to do, not what we wanted. In grade eight he was put in a grade 7/8 split class. There were only 4 other grade eights in this class. He took it as a personal insult and has never been the same happy go lucky kid since. Grade nine came with rebellion. After failing a class in grade nine we thought that he had learned his lesson and would put more effort into his next year. We have tried to stay off his back, like he has asked, but now he has received his marks from the first half of the term and he has only one mark that is over 60. He has asked us again today, to stay off his back. I told him that our trying to do this obviously didn't work. I also told him that I loved him and wanted do right by him and if that meant helping him to organize his time to complete his tasks, than that was what I would do. I am confused as to whether I should just let him go ahead and walk all over us by leaving him to do as he pleases or tighten things up more by being tougher. We have tried the reward system i.e.; get up everyday and get yourself to school on time and you can go out on the week-ends. He says that as a result he hates school. He used to be such an easy going guy, we can't pinpoint what has happened and we are

very concerned that he may really hurt himself along the
way.

Lightning Source UK Ltd.
Milton Keynes UK
UKOW051938240213

206748UK00001B/17/P

9 781601 452627